AN

Plowmen's Clocks

ALISON UTTLEY

Plowmen's Clocks

When shepherds pipe on oaten straws,
And merry larks are plowmen's clocks

Illustrated by
C. F. TUNNICLIFFE

FABER & FABER LTD
24 Russell Square
London

First published in mcmlii
by Faber and Faber Limited
24 Russell Square, London, W.C.1
Printed in Great Britain by
Western Printing Services Limited, Bristol

Contents

Kitchens

'In the castle kitchen a great fire was blazing and Halvor went in, but such a kitchen he had never seen in all his born days. It was so grand and fine; there were vessels of silver and vessels of gold, but still never a living soul. So when Halvor had stood there a while and no one came out, he went and opened a door, and there inside sat a Princess who span upon a spinning-wheel.'

I looked round the room and pondered these words, and I was filled with bliss, for there I was like Halvor at Soria Moria Castle, alone in the kitchen. The three doors were shut, and the place was all mine, in a silence I seldom experienced. I did not want to read any more, I was already enchanted, living a secret life of my own. I sat in the corner of the settle, sharing life with the inanimate, listening to all the intimate sounds which filled the air, sounds which I could never hear when others were present, looking at all the well-known objects which took on a new expression, revealing something I had not seen before. If I opened one of the doors, I might see the Princess spinning at her wheel, as once my grandmother spun there. If I opened the second door, there might be a frightful apparition waiting for me. If I opened the third door, I should find a beggar with a sack on his back, or Long John Silver, or Robinson Crusoe. I sat very still, in Soria Moria Castle.

It was the friendly homely little kitchen, the dwelling-place of the spirit of the house, the axis around which the rest revolved. It was the refuge from ghost and terror and goblin hands, the rock of security, where we said our prayers kneeling on the stone floor. It was the room where someone cooked and baked and another made butter, where sewing and mending were done, and a child could play with her toys and a weary man could sleep, and a lamb could be weaned with a bottle of milk and all sick and tired and unhappy ones could be comforted and restored to new health.

Silence, with never a human voice, for my mother was upstairs and my father and little brother were out in the fields, and the servant was somewhere—so I grasped the moment out of eternity to myself and held it and absorbed its length and breadth and thickness.

Silence, but the room was filled with small sounds which I could hear. The grandfather clock ticked more loudly, speaking to me with insistent words. He was safe in his oak case, but his shining brass face with the cupids in the corners winked at me in the firelight, and the bull's-eye glass blinked, speaking of the past, and the future, foretelling and prophesying until I turned my head refusing to hear any more. He talked too much.

I heard the faint creak of the best harness which hung on the wall, and the smell of the leather traces and reins reminded me of the stable and horses. Feathers in the cushions, behind me, spices on the dresser, rainwater in the tap, all gave out their strong odours to the room. There was the smell of heat, the smell of old things, the smell of stone, and new bread and rainwater and moss.

The fire crackled, and called for more coal, the meat in the oven sizzled behind the iron door, and the flies talked interminably as they circled round the low ceiling. The tap was dripping with a clear bright ring as the rainwater fell in a lade-can, and the musical sound rose and fell like a cadence, sweet as a harp. A mouse nibbled among the boots under the frill of the settle, hesitating, and then starting afresh, and a monthly rose dropped its pink petals with a flurry of soft snow on the table. The armchair creaked, as if someone were sitting there, and a round shallow basket on the hearth-stone actually moved a fraction to escape the fire's heat. Everything had life, and I sat there listening, watching the old kitchen as Helvor watched the enchanted kitchen in the fairy tale of Soria Moria Castle.

Through the window poured the pure clear light of the hills, and the fields were freckled with sunshine and shadow as the clouds raced down from the north. The giant picture of the house lay on the slope of the nearest field, a dark blue mysterious shadowy house, but the light belonged to the hills and sky and could not enter those layers of darkness.

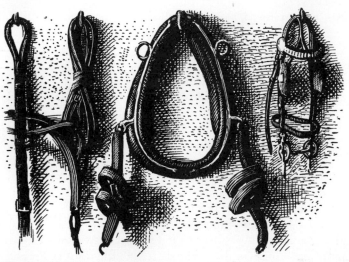

The kitchen had its own source of brightness, its own sun shone from the bars of the fire, and the firelight was reflected from copper and brass which hung round the room. It was so vividly alive with the dazzling flecks of light, one could imagine a musical sound came from the illuminated starry points. The room was laughing to itself and I heard it.

Silence in the kitchen, and nobody entered. Surely the spell would be broken before anything had time to happen. The room was rarely left to itself, there was always someone opening a door to peep at the clock, to look in the oven, to get a bucket of hot water, or simply to walk from one door to another.

'It was so grand and fine; there were vessels of silver and vessels of gold, but still never a living soul.'

Yes, it was grand and fine, and it was not poor and homely, thought I as I considered it with awakened eyes, for gold and silver were all over the place. The milk cans shone like silver in their corners, and the row of spice tins on the dresser were silver too, they were so bright. I let my eyes rove along the dresser where the painted dinner service was displayed. The plates were ranged along the shelves symmetrically with the sauce-boats on their stands in the centre, and the great meat dishes on high. The crooked brown trees on the deep soup plates, the flying green-winged birds of paradise, with tufts on their heads, the peonies and water-lilies and butterflies, with the green and cerise border of flowers made a fine pattern up there. It was a service for the Princess who sat at her wheel. All the terracotta jugs with faces on their handles and bearded heads on their spouts pleased my senses. They were smooth, and warm, the jugs held no reflections, they were brown, earthy possessions which had always been there, with a life of their own, aware of me, aware of all things, not in heaven and earth, but in earth and the underworld.

The oak dresser which held them would have delighted Halvor, and he might have sat on its beeswaxed top, where men often leaned as they talked. It was the correct height for a seat, but only the best people were allowed to rest there. No inferior person dare sit on that polished surface, next to the oak spoon-box, the knife-box, and the rows of spice-boxes and big old pincushion and family Bible. Halvor might have opened one of the three drawers, with their intricate and beautiful brass handles, and he would have seen story books hidden among starched white neatly-folded linen aprons, and the blotter from the insurance company, and paper and envelopes ready for letters. My fairy-tale book came from one drawer and there was the scent of starched linen and lad's-love in its pages, while a pressed pansy marked my place.

Against the other wall was the second dresser, with many painted drawers and a white linen tablecloth over its top. Nobody could sit there. It was laden with feminine things, the baby basket of childhood, which now held the mending, an inlaid mahogany work-box, the brass-cornered mahogany writing desk with bills and sealing wax and stamps in the little drawers, and in the centre of the dresser stood the ancient bronze tea-urn, with a bearded face of a satyr on the spout. There were many strange faces on jugs and tea-pots and mugs; men with slanting eyes and little horns on their heads stared from pot and pan, winking and blinking as they had done for a hundred years, but the most wicked faces looked out from the tea urn, from the round handles and the little tap which turned to pour out innocent tea at Mothers' Meetings.

All these faces came to life, they whispered and watched, and they knew far too much. I washed them when they were dirty, and gazed at the curling hair, and the horns on their heads. I knew nothing of satyrs and fauns, but they seemed to be akin to the light and shadows of the great woods, when I felt that some other life was going on, a primitive evocation very close to me. They had no power in the kitchen, where they were captured in the earthenware and china, but outside it was a different matter.

Above the second dresser hung vessels of silver. At least they were as bright as silver, they were plated, and polished to a perfection, for they were my mother's pride, as they had been my father's mother's. Halvor, on entering Soria Moria Castle, would certainly have thought the row of dish-covers was solid silver. They were important, they were part of the secret life, they each held a picture of the room in their convex surfaces, and I could see myself there, very small in the distance as they hung like seven mirrors on the wall opposite the fire. The largest was never used, and I thought it was a shield Roman soldiers might have used in battle. It was a giant, but the second in size covered

a twenty-pound sirloin, or a quarter of lamb, and the smallest one was used for kidneys on toast. Their central handles were surrounded with leaves, and they hung by triangular loops of metal. Dish-covers were part of every kitchen, and once when I was allowed to peer into the great kitchen of the Squire's castle, I saw similar ones on his wall.

The vessels of gold were the brass and copper saucepans on the shelf over my head. The bright metal, polished with bath-brick, winked up there in the shadows. They caught the light from the fire and sent it back with pin-points of glitter. The brass candlesticks on the mantel-piece, the copper kettle and the Sheffield mugs, all added to the vessels of gold and silver in the room.

Hooks in the ceiling were an important part of kitchen economy of space. From our big hooks, embedded in beams, hung hams and shoulders of bacon, which were curing in the winter months. There was a gun across two hooks, and the best lantern with cut-glass windows for going to church hung on another, with a little jolly lantern which I took to school on the next. The bird cage hung where everyone could talk to the canary, and a bunch of herbs hung near it. Even an antique birch-rod hung from a hook, and a truncheon weighted with lead. In the centre over the table was the big lamp, with white shade, ready for night. Whips stood in a corner by the grandfather clock, with walking sticks and ramrod and a rifle. When the wind blew hard through the house, rushing in from the hills at the exposed north door, and leaving at the sheltered south, all the hanging objects swayed to and fro, as if they were in a

ship's cabin, but I remembered the house was built on bare rock, with foundations going into the heart of the earth. We were safe, we couldn't be blown down.

The kitchen table took up a good part of the floor, and it was the centre-piece of the room, with clean smooth top, scrubbed every day to a snowy whiteness, that was covered in the evening with a tasselled blue and red cloth. Its broad base and stout legs held it firmly, and it was laden all morning with food being prepared. Fowls and rabbits, meat and pastry board were here, pancheons for bread-making, and the churn for butter-making.

I learned many things in that busy room, packed with life and experience, for the senses of children are acutely perceptive, and, though I was reading a fairy-tale book, with my fingers in my ears to keep out the human voices, as distinct from the tiny sibilant sounds I always heard, although I was later lost in the wonders of light and electricity, I was unconsciously absorbing the way of life around me. I looked up from my book, but everything went on just the same, and I got glimpses of hard work into which I was unwillingly drawn, of baking and cooking, and bread-making, or the dressing of fowls, and making of butter, of the preparation of many meals. Out of the corner of my eye, as I dreamed of magical happenings, of fairy and invisible worlds, of Queen Elizabeth and Queen Mab, I saw all the cooking of a busy household, with visitors coming and going; I saw kettles and saucepans mended and soldered, with the soldering iron heated in the fire, and the silvery stick of solder held over the little hole. I saw wood carved into little shapes of boats and dolls and tops to amuse us. I saw whistles and pipes made, and I joined in the music. I knew instinctively the processes of farm life, the feeding of the cade lamb deserted by its mother, the preparation of food for man and beast, and I heard country wisdom, that animals must always be looked after before one thought of oneself, that no burden that was too heavy should be laid upon them, there should be mercy as we also hoped for mercy. All was part of the life in the farm kitchen, and, when I was older and I sat in another room to do my work in solitude, I missed this old wisdom of earth.

Silently I sat in the shadows, reading with waves of firelight and darkness thrown over my book, as people passed between me and the lamp. Silently I lived in two worlds, one of fairytale and poetry, the other of country happenings.

Long afterwards I found I had remembered these things, these methods of cooking and baking and housewifery, from the bird's-eye glance I took from my fairy book. The mixing of herbs, the ways of cooking and serving and living were engrained in my own life, an unconscious absorption. I remembered the labour of the fields, the richness of the earth, the luck of the gun, the harvest of orchard and garden which had contributed to the kitchen and its simple wealth.

More than anywhere else in the house, there was this feeling of continuity about the kitchen, where generations had lived, a room which seemed to exist in four dimensions, space and time itself, as the earth rolled round and the house and rock upon which it stood moved with it through time.

'So when Halvor had stood there a while and no one came out, he went and opened a door, and there inside sat a Princess who span upon a spinning-wheel.'

✺ II ✺

Fires

One of the most primitive pleasures and absorbing miracles of early life, and indeed of all time, was a fire —a kitchen fire, a bedroom fire, a parlour fire, a bonfire, a blaze in a pasture when men were hedging, even a fire crackling under the copper in the brewhouse when clothes were bouncing up and down in the hot water.

The upward rush of flames antlered like a golden stag, or plumed like the wings of a rare gold bird, made a splendid scene; the crackle and whisper and low murmur of fire voices was a background of invisible creatures, carrying on their private conversation, talking of this and that together, and comforting the humble listeners, because the intonation was soft and homely, a dialect which country people could understand.

The fire which lighted the room so that only a couple of candles was needed beside it, the fire which talked and sang and whispered, was a living entity. It was an animal, dwelling with us, sharing our life, chained like a great gold bear to the iron bars of the fireplace. It was kept in order with a long poker, and fed with bucketfuls of fuel, and admired and praised for its blazing tongues that licked the bars.

When my mother read aloud an old German folk tale of Herr Bruin who came out of the wilds and pushed open the door to live as one with the family in the woods, we thought he was our fire, who had come to share our life. I heard the pad pad of his soft feet on the stones, the rustle of his fur like snow against the door-posts, as he pushed inside the kitchen. Then he went

18

into the great yellow cave of the fire, and stayed there to tell us tales on winter nights.

Sometimes he lived in the dining-room, where we had enormous fires in the winter, made of logs of wood from fallen trees, and lumps of shining coal, backed with slack to keep the fire quiet during the day. When night fell and the shutters were closed, before the candles were lighted, someone poked the smouldering heap and in a flash the flames darted up, the fire opened out to disclose golden caves with roofs and pillars and such hot interiors we dare not look too closely. All fairy tale, all poetry, all magical things lived within those caverns. We read by the light of the fire and sewed in its blaze, while shadows danced on the ceiling, and stars flickered on the furniture and pictures.

When I seek in the depths of memory those early childhood feelings, visiting rooms I once knew, I see first of all the fire. I always stand on the threshold of a doorway and look at the fire. Then I go forward in imagination and everything is remembered with a glow upon it, darkly shadowed or candle-lit, but lighted by the fire on the hearth, which burned winter and summer. Little attics that had no fireplace, barns and stables, cowhouses and sheds, all are seen in exact detail as if a photograph had been taken at some unknown time, but I do not linger. I hurry down the stone stairways, I fling open a door and gaze hungrily at the fire which gives life to the house. This visual image is so clear, I am warmed as I raise it out of the depths and enter a life once lived. Then illuminated faces come from the shadows and people welcome me and I am free to wander wherever I desire.

There was the kitchen fire, the most royal and grand, tended with religious care, for it was the core of the house. Upon its heat might depend life and death. Fire meant hot water in the sudden emergencies of a farm, it meant warmth for a sick animal, and a chilled man whose heart was frozen. On the broad hearthstone, sanded to a rich golden yellow with a lump of stone from the hill, and kept immaculately clean, the flames beat down with life-giving strength. The round plaited basket with a sickly chicken lay there, covered with a cloth, or a bird someone had found hurt, or a newborn lamb weak and struggling for new life, or dough rising in a yellow pancheon. All were given life. Close to the hearth sat the man who had come home from a journey white-lipped after driving in the icy winds, eyes blinking back the water. Snow and frost, wild gales and heavy rain, all might do their worst, but there was that glorious fire to think of during the long drive home.

I came home from school, often wet to the skin with the beating rain on the exposed hills, but there was always the heart of the fire to bring back colour and health. As I walked through the dark woods I concentrated my thoughts on the fire at the end of my journey, and the image of it has stayed there in my mind for all the years. I sat on a low stool on the hearthrug, not too close to the blaze, but near enough to warm my body. When I was very young, I was undressed there, and wrapped in a blanket, and my coat was hung in the brewhouse to drip on the floor. This was security, and home and love, a picture I take with me wherever I go.

The room always seemed to be filled with people and shadows and light, with happenings and talk and cheerful noise of men coming through the outside doors, but the voices were amicable, seldom raised in angry altercation. Children had to be seen and not heard, so we listened to the talk and picked up threads of the pattern which had been woven in the country life, as we warmed ourselves on the hearth.

In front of the fire, resting on a trivet fastened to the bars, was the Dutch oven, bright as silver, with perhaps lamb chops dangling from little hooks, or beef-steak grilling there, or a piece of home-made cheese toasting, ready for the important meal after milking was done. The fire beat on the hearth, on the little Dutch oven with its savoury food, on the faces of men and women, and there was a rosy glow over all.

On the top of the fire was the big copper kettle containing two or three gallons of water, simmering and humming to itself. By its side was the middle-sized copper kettle, which held a gallon, likewise steaming and bubbling, ready for tea. Near, over the oven, was the enormous copper-pan, which held the supply of hot water for animals' food and the scalding of milk churns and utensils. These three vessels sang in little voices, all of a different pitch, like a choir, and they mingled gently with the voices of the farmhouse, and the mysterious song that always was there in my ears, the murmur of the fire.

The fire, king of the busy room, crackled and sparkled on frosty nights, and roared in the chimney with a noise of thunder, as the wind caught it and carried it away.

It burned coal at an astonishing rate and there were many headshakes over its extravagance, but it warmed an entire household, it kept the wheels of life oiled, and it saved life by its power and beneficence. Many years later, when a new modern range was put in for reasons of economy and easy cleaning, there was a sad change, and the wind called in vain to the flames.

Winter and summer the fire burned with cheerful wastefulness, but in the hot days of harvesting and jam-making it was over-powering, and the tinsmith in the village made a screen to ward off the heat. It was a folding screen of bright tin mounted on wooden panels. We were astonished that the clean white metal which held a moving picture of the dancing flames was itself cold, and we learned the lesson of heat reflection.

The fire was the laboratory for scientific experiment. We secreted chemicals at school and threw them on the flames to see the colours. Scarlet, blue, violet they shone. We filled a churchwarden pipe with coal dust, stopped it with clay from the fields, and heated it to burn the escaping coal gas. We burned empty cartridges and watched the peacock colours of the powder crumbs. It was very interesting to inquiring minds, but we were forbidden to use the long poker or tongs of ancient shape. Indeed they were as big as ourselves, and they stayed in their corner, sacred to the firemakers. The leather bellows too were not for us, although we could use the brass poker and various implements in the dining-room, where there were broad brass fenders on the stone floor.

The fire was the object of various superstitions, which I heard from my earliest days. Everyone who came added to the store of tales, as they sat by the blaze and stared into the golden caves. Something there reminded them, something stirred their minds, and out came an antique memory, preceded by 'I've heard say as . . .'

The little flag of soot which hung on the bars was the symbol of a stranger, firmly believed, and so quickly followed by reality, there seemed to be no doubt of its truth. The fire was warning us of someone already on the way, down in the valley, or driving along the road, clip-clopping, to the bottom of the hill, or walking steadfastly to give us a surprise. People did not write to say they were coming, they came, for we were always at home, and there was plenty of food and warmth and a bed. If the soot blew off, then the visit had been postponed, we thought.

Cinders sometimes shot from the fire down to the hearth, and these were regarded by the maid with keen curiosity, although the rest of the family refused to acknowledge any portent here. She whispered to me, and with wide eyes I examined the tiny things. One was a coffin, and one a purse of gold. I hoped a purse would fly from the fire for my own spending, but the significance of the coffin I did not apprehend.

Coal was part of the kitchen itself, and glossy black lumps filled a couple of scuttles on the left of the hearth, shining pieces, bright as if polished. It was bought by the truck, and ordered from the pithead, where it had been hewn from the deep earth. The truck was left at a railway siding a few miles away, from which the coal was fetched by the wharf coal carts, drawn by splendid horses with brasses on their faces, and bells

on their heads. We sent an extra horse down the hill to help them pull the loads up the long steep winding road to the house. It was cheaper to buy the coal in this manner, for it came from the coal-mines over the hills of our county, it was dug out by colliers, and we heard tales of the mines and the workings.

When the coal-carts came round the sudden corner, the last bend to the top, we ran out to see the sight. The barking dog was shut in the stable, and the carts were drawn across the yard to the coal-house, and backed through the great doorway. There was a roar of falling coal, and the men were given drinks of ale out in the yard.

When they had gone, and all was quiet, we went to see the

shining black lumps, which were very large indeed. They looked so clean and polished we were surprised that our hands were blackened by them. The lad built them up against the wall, for they were as big as the blocks of stone which formed that

ancient part of the house. The coalhouse, open to the sky, had buttressed walls, ivy-covered, which rose from the rocky hillside like castle walls. It was a very old part of the farm, very romantic to me, and I climbed the lumps, laid like a staircase, and peered over the rampart of thick wall to the woods below and the land falling steeply in that rocky place. I could see down across the valley, and over the tops of trees, to the glittering lovely river, while close to my face were the rich ivy tods with their clustering purple berries.

The coal was examined closely for fossil ferns and leaves, for gold pyrites and flecks of silver. When the lad split the blocks asunder and filled the scuttles we looked for treasure of the coal age, expecting to find something rare and beautiful.

The coal lay in great blocks as it had been hewn out of the earth, clear and fresh, and exciting, as if it too were surprised to find itself out in the open air of the hill-top, instead of in the depths of the earth.

The servant lad carried a lump in his two hands, across the yard, in at the kitchen, for the dining-room fire. Straight across the hall he went, and the piece was placed in the circular grate, on the flaming mass, 'To last a long time'. It burned for hours, with bright flames of orange and gold playing about its head. Then, when it was hollowed, and night had come, and the time for fairy books or novels, according to our age and taste, we stared into the golden caverns to discover something, to find a castle with pillars and halls and turrets. Only a great fire in an old grate could hold those enchanted palaces, which were part of childhood. I think I gazed into the caves and flickering golden places of the fire as children nowadays watch the television screen, and perhaps I saw more in those mysterious rooms. I saw stories acted before my eyes, in that glowing coal which had tradition behind it, our native coal from our own county.

It was dug by colliers, black-faced men, who had a romantic air about them when I occasionally saw them. They had whippets and they carried Davy lamps, I was told. They were brave and wild and terrible. Many a story was told about the colliers who went deep into the earth, under the forests where Robin Hood perhaps once hunted. The earth itself, with its caves and swallet holes, its hidden springs, its lead mines and coal-mines, its quarries and fossils and strangely shaped rocks was a source of delight and fear and imagination. Dwarfs, gnomes, elves lived there, like the bear in the fire and we might see one of these immortals if we were quick to catch them.

Fires were the source of happenings, for with people hovering around it, a fire conceals some of its mystery. Alone, the flames seemed to call forth all the invisible life of the house. Fancy was free to roam in a room with firelight and candlelight and solitude, and I often retreated with my books. In one room in particular, where I sat with lesson and story books, there was such a flurry of ghosts and merriment, of information given and received that as soon as I entered and carried the tall silver candlestick from the mantelpiece to the table, something happened, and I felt a different being. Shutters were fastened across the three windows, thick curtains were drawn over the shutters, and the house came to life. A comfort flooded me. I felt the security of thick walls, and stout oak, and peace of mind. I was safe from battle, murder and sudden death. I was safe from want and mockery, safe from the perils and dangers of this night. I read Keats and Goldsmith, *King Solomon's Mines* and

She. They were all true, for the fire induced truth. The words were alive, they swung around me, like music and eternity. The birds on the curtains moved their wings and the flames of the fire joined in the liveliness.

Out-of-doors the fire under the hedge, when old John the hedge-cutter had slashed the branches and set alight the great heaps of thorny cuttings, made a comforting sight. It brought home to the fields, as if the world were suddenly made into a bedroom, with roof of blue sky, and walls of thorn, and fire burning there. The old man boiled his blue can of tea on the embers, and drank from the cup-lid, and we took a sip of the strong bitter-sweet brew. He ate his bread with the thick slice of cold bacon, while we piled more branches on the fire. In the field, under an oak tree, lay a great bough which had fallen in the autumn gales. It would be sawn up for the house fires, to set the sparks flying and the flames dancing, but the masses of crooked twigs and smaller branches were fed to the hedge-cuttings and thrown on the fire under the sky.

There was the good-smelling fire of the potato haulms, when the crop in the plough-field had been lifted and stored, although this was often a smouldering affair after the first blaze, and we left others to tend it. Our own private fire was the bonfire for Guy Fawkes, in the corner of the plough-field, when the year's accumulation of letters and papers was brought in crates from the brewhouse bench, and turned over with the scurry of mice who had made a home in it. The paper was heaped over the foundation of sticks and then we built up a mountain of branches dragged from the fields and edges of the woods. When darkness came and the stars were out we lighted the vast pile, and shouted and sang as the blaze swept up towards the sky. Faces in the glow had a strange look, as if we were all savages, dancing round a cannibal feast. It was exhilarating, and beautiful out there with the shadows and the darting bats aroused from sleep in the old apple tree hollow. Yet it was sad, as the fire burned low, and people drifted back to the house. Like Christmas, it was once a year, and there was always a feeling of

sorrow when it was over, and only a ring of ashes with a few fragments of rockets and fireworks showed what had once been a golden tree of many branches.

Now again winter is coming, and fires are lighted. There is no glorious kitchen fire to warm the heart of my house, only a dark boiler, and bedrooms are heated with electricity, but there is one big fireplace in my sitting-room where a wood fire burns. I carry little branches from the small beech wood, and pile them on the logs of wood to sparkle and crackle and sing. The stronger the wind, the more furious the gale, the happier I am, for I know that the dead branches will come crashing down in the wood and I can watch for the enticing shadows which hide in the corners of the room, waiting for the fire to bring them out.

III

Summer Holidays

Holidays were never very important to us because we did not expect them. Nobody asked the embarrassing question 'Where are you going this year?' and we were saved from confessing that we were not going away at all. Why should we go away? It was not the accepted tradition for children to be rushed off to the sea. It cost too much money, it was something out of our way of life. Visitors came to us for their holidays, children stayed at the farm, and we had companions for cricket and hide-and-seek. To go away ourselves, except to stay with relations, was unnecessary. We lived in a healthy place, we needed no change of air.

Sometimes I went to the house of my mother's friends, where there was a stiffness and sobriety in the atmosphere which froze me. I was lonely and desperate to get home again, but I had to stay the appointed time. Sometimes I stayed with school friends, but always there were grown-up people whose outlook was so different from mine. These short visits could hardly be called 'holidays', and I was always glad to return home to the haymaking and country delights of the farm.

When I got back I looked around suspiciously, wondering what I had missed, and I went along the hedges and walls seeking flowers and birds which might have appeared without my knowledge. I peered into barns for new implements, a fork with a white handle, a besom, a hay-rake, and into calf-place and cow-house for strangers. It was not wise to be too long away, when there were cricket matches down in the valley, and Irish labourers with their romantic odours of twist and Ireland walking the fields, and haymaking every day, and nights of songs under the stars. I had to keep watch or some pages of life might be turned without my reading them.

However, there was one holiday a year which belonged to our family, although only two or three times did I share it, for it had nothing to do with me. It was talked of for months, with money put aside for the purpose, small savings and windfalls. It was a dazzling ten days at Blackpool.

Ten days! There was magic in that number—a period over a week but less than a fortnight, and I always wondered why it was exactly ten, until years later I realized it was a ten-day excursion, which cost very little. This visit of my father to the great town by the sea was his garland of the year, which he wore with pride. He stored his mind with the splendours of the dashing waves and the circus, he breathed in the salty air, and came back with tales to last for the next eleven months.

He had worked for this holiday and earned it, every penny, and the money was kept in his painted chest in the attic. One did not draw from the bank for a holiday. If we had had heavy losses then my mother contrived by most rigid economies to make up for it somehow. Only the direst calamity stopped his ten days. This yearly relaxation was something which was his due. The immense bodily labour of the fields in storm and snow, when hands were bleeding and raw with frosts and the senses numb with cold, the long days of harvest when men worked from dawn to starlight, sweating and weary but never giving way as they strove to gather the hay in the shortest time before rain fell and ruined it—this labour which had its own repayment in the joys of conquering nature, had to receive a crown. For some the reward was Wakes Week, when the Fair came to the village and the hobby horses, shooting booths and the stalls with brandy snap and horehound sweets made life a holiday, but this was for the young and irresponsible and poor. My father was going to Blackpool and everybody knew, for we talked about it with pride.

My mother occasionally went with him, but a farm cannot be left without someone in authority to govern the little kingdom of animals and helpers. Blackpool with its garish attractions had no allure for her quiet spirit, although she was glad to go anywhere with my father. Later on she stayed with her friends, and took her pleasures in their gentle company. Not so my father, who had known solitude and loneliness for a year. He wanted a change of environment and air. He wanted town for country, with the mighty ocean for green fields, and the society of strangers instead of animals. My brother often went with him, and once or twice I joined the company, a dazzled, bewildered girl.

There were great preparations for this holiday, which came in the autumn when the harvest was over and school had begun. Sometimes our old retired farm man, Josiah, came to stay with us to help the servant lad with milking, or an aged uncle came to the house. An elderly woman came in my mother's place, if she too went away, someone who accepted the position of trust as a holiday for herself.

Once when my mother and father went away together we

had a staid religious woman to look after us. She was perhaps thirty but I thought of her as at least seventy, for she had a long face and forbidding manner. Each night when the work was done, and we had played dominoes and beggar-my-neighbour, she began to prophesy. I sat in the kitchen, ostensibly reading a fairy book, but listening with growing apprehension to her conversation with the servant lad. She discussed the end of the world and the imminence of that event, drawing on the Bible with such convincing argument, I was stiff with fear, but fascinated too.

The young man listened intently, impressed by her eloquence and I used to go to bed with my lighted candle wondering if the world would end in the night. A host of apparitions accompanied me. Saints and martyrs were the familiars of this young woman, and I was thankful when my parents returned safely before the last trump sounded and the graves gave up their dead.

When letters had been written and our guardians chosen, there was the room to be re-engaged in the Blackpool boarding house, and clothes to be cleaned with ammonia and pressed and the portmanteau fetched from the attic. Sundays suits and fresh garments were aired and packed. We smelled the aroma of herbs and hayseeds and pomatum in my father's clothes, of lavender and something delicate and elusive in my mother's, a scent which still haunts old workboxes.

A little store of food was prepared—half a ham and some delicacies for their Blackpool friends, a minister who had retired to the seaside from our village, and a basket of new-laid eggs for the landlady. She would expect a present from the farm, they said. Her own speciality was rice-pudding, very sweet, with nutmeg grated over the surface.

Before they left there was a great cooking, for those left behind. Rabbit pies and apple tarts, jam puffs and cakes and pasties were made and stored on the dairy shelves, so that we should have enough to eat. Farm work was planned, the household affairs arranged, and there were endless directions about keeping animals warm and shutting cowhouse doors and field gates, guarding against foxes and poachers, and writing letters.

I looked forward to doing exactly what I wanted while they were away, but I soon longed for their return. The house felt lonely in its silence and even the dog and the horses missed them.

At Blackpool each important day was packed with new experiences for the country people. My father stood and gazed at the crowds on the promenades and piers, proud to be one of them, and he wondered at their numbers as they came pouring from the stations, thronging the streets even in the autumn.

'Where they all come from I don't know', he would remark, but my mother would retreat and try to find a quiet spot.

He was aware of his own individuality in the great world of humanity. He took with him his serenity and good humour, and I think he must have been a striking figure with his square top hat, his massive form, as he stood like a rock in the flood of townsfolk.

He went to the Tower circus and menagerie, to Wesleyan chapel and revival meeting and Sunday concert, to conjurers and magicians, but not to theatres or church. He knew nothing of plays and he couldn't find his way in the prayer-book alone. He rejoiced at the sea, especially when the storms raged and great waves dashed over the promenade, and he walked on a pier each day, but he never went in a boat, or sat on the beach. Placidly he visited the lions and elephants in the wild beast shows, and compared them with the beasts in the little circuses that came to the village now and then. He treasured up the sayings of the clowns and the ventriloquists. Once when we all went to Blackpool we had our 'bumps' felt by a phrenologist, and we firmly believed every word those sooth-sayers wrote down in the little white books of our lives. Years later I came across these books, and I was astonished at the truth in them.

At the end of the holiday there was a shopping expedition to buy presents for those left at home, and for my brother's

birthday, which happily coincided with the visit. My brother chose a volume of *Chums*, or a cricket bat, and I too had asked for a book, *The Last Days of Pompeii*, or *Ben Hur*, in a seven-penny edition, with poor print and cheap paper.

There was a remarkable shop as different as possible from our little village shops with their small windows and steps down to the floor and jangling bells. It was a bazaar of toys and

gifts, and the building was decorated with flags and lanterns. Part of this great store had sevenpenny articles, but a select portion was set aside for gifts at half-a-crown and five shillings.

The objects of my desire when I went there, and my choice when I was at home, were shell-covered boxes, hair-brushes with shells on the back, mirrors with surrounds of shells, purses, and pictures framed in shells. I could never see enough of these wonderful things. They fascinated me so deeply that I lingered to gaze at them instead of looking at the sea. I thought they came from the floor of the ocean, where perhaps the mermaids lived, and these little hand-glasses and trinket-boxes with their exquisite amber and yellow shells, their mother-of-pearl and lavender spirals and involutes might have been held in a mermaid's hand. I always chose a shell souvenir for my present if there was enough money for it. It was a constant surprise that my mother did not share my ravishment by these many-coloured opalescent sea-shells.

When the family came home we sat breathlessly waiting for the portmanteau to be unpacked and the presents disclosed. Sometimes there was a humming-top with tunes in its lid, or a small musical-box, and a sixpenny sheet of music. Perhaps a silver brooch with my name on it, or a bead necklace or a silver bangle was there, with the shell-box or shell-purse. Blackpool

rock came for everybody, with words imbedded under the rosy skin, so that at every bite we could read it afresh. We always looked to see if it were still there. There was a bag of 'pebbles', sweets mottled and grey like the stones on the beach, and a piece of sea-weed to be hung from a hook in the kitchen, to foretell the weather.

One year my father brought home a pair of atrocious vases which he gave my mother with great satisfaction. She never flinched, she kept her dismay to herself as she thanked him, and she put them in the place of honour among pieces of Derby china and treasures of the past, where they always rested.

There were tales to be told, and all the adventures of the travellers to be related many times. Even my father was glad to be home, thankful that the noise of the crowds was left behind. The quietness and peace of the country filled his heart, but he had a faint regret for one thing.

'They'll just be going in at the Circus now', he would say, looking wistfully at the grandfather clock ticking solemnly in its corner. The owl hooted and called in the great trees, the dog barked restlessly and the horse in the stable stamped his hoof.

Lions and tigers prowled across the lawn, clowns turned

somersaults, and tight-rope dancers swung over the orchard on the clothes-line. Elephants trumpeted in the yard and the circus-master cracked his whip.

We sat by the fire with our new books and toys, and we listened. The lamp made a little warm circle of radiance, and the fire blazed and crackled as the wind swept from the hills. Black shadows came trooping out of the corners of the room, eager to hear the talk of circus and trapeze artiste and raging sea. Even the stones of the house itself wakened up when my father told about his holiday.

IV

Travelling

Along the country roads came a slow cavalcade of traffic, which interested us profoundly as we sat in the spring cart, holding the reins, waiting for my father. We watched this procession with wide intent eyes, unaware that all the passing vehicles which we thought so splendid were passing in time as well as in space. It was a colourful pageant of country life we were witnessing, a display for the end of an era. Yet if we had been told of racing cars, and aeroplanes and motor-buses and lorries, we should not have been surprised, for our minds were open to receive anything in heaven or earth, and we fully expected that before we were full grown we should have mechanical wings to fly from place to place. We read Jules Verne, and H. G. Wells, and the schoolmaster himself had a little red car that tooted as he drove along. The castle still kept the carriages and horses, the coachman with his cockaded hat, and the grooms. In a motor-car they could not travel in such state, and we wondered what would happen in the future, but our attention was on the present.

There was a brake, a four-wheeled open vehicle, with a load of passengers, going on a sight-seeing tour. On the step at the back stood a glorious man in fine scarlet coat, who blew a horn to make echoes against the rocks. Two pairs of horses galloped with this magnificent vehicle, and we stood up to see them pass. We watched the people, whose glances fell on the tossing river, on the rocks, on the scenery and waterfall, and we felt proud that we belonged, while they were strangers.

Sometimes the horn was long and straight, sometimes curly

like a ram's horn, but always it gave us a shiver of delight. We could hear the sound from far away, across the valley when we were at home, but when we were down on the turnpike it was a glorious sight to see this turnout with the fine horses and sparkling brake and driver with his ribbons held proudly as he went along the valley road.

Next came the water-cart, the green painted cart and its

fountain of water. This was an important and somewhat disconcerting approach, for, if the water-man did not turn off the fountain as he passed us, the pony would take fright and gallop away. Nervously we held on, with one hand clutching the handle of the ratchet which controlled the brake, and the other holding the reins. Nothing happened, the water was switched low, the fountain trickled away and the cart passed us safely. Then, on came the water, and the many little fountains curved out to form a large fan which watered the limestone dust and laid it flat on the road, so that it would not rise up in a cloud. The smell of it was utterly delicious, it was like moss and wet places, ferns and limestone, springs and toadstools. We wrinkled our noses in delight, and envied the man on the water-cart who had such power and glory, who could create a fountain, and turn it off. The sun-rays made a rainbow in the water, and the water-man seemed like Apollo, with his fountain and rainbow following him obediently, turning when he turned, while birds flew down to bathe in the wet dust. Sometimes we had the felicity of seeing the water-cart filled, for one of our stopping-places when out driving was the fish-pond. While my father went to the fishmonger, Mr Wildgoose, whose open-fronted shop was conveniently near the pond, we could watch the water-cart draw into the yard of the coaching stables and suck up the green water. The pond was stocked with goldfish and a few languid water-lilies grew on the surface. Everyone leaned over the railing to watch the fish, and later a penny-in-the-slot machine with fish-food was hung near. In the centre of the little pond was a small fountain, a primitive thing, but it played and sent up a thin trickle to dance in the sunshine. Around the edge were stones with hart's-tongue ferns cunningly arranged as if they had always grown there instead of in the woods we knew so well.

We stood on the bottom rail, and gazed at the goldfish, at the fountain, and the water-cart, all in the coaching yard, where men were busy with horses, and the sound of the river below filled the air with murmurings.

We heard the tinkle of bells and a cart came past, with a set of harness bells that rang merrily as the horse shook his head and ambled along. It was a vegetable cart, laden with carrots and apples, drawn by a poor old horse, but the bells set in the frame on the hames gave a cheerful sound. People stopped and patted the horse and talked to him. We too had a bell, round and silvered, and the tinkle was clear and mellow. It made an accompaniment to the trotting of the pony's hooves on the hard road, and the clatter of the wheels. When the pony shook his head the bell rang loudly and warned the driver, who was perhaps in a shop, to hurry out. These round bells were called 'Rumblers', or 'Crotals'. One could hear the sweet tinkle in the lanes and round the corners as horses approached.

We were always interested in the trappings of the horses we

saw, the colours of the head-bands, the variety of the horse-brasses, the decorated whips with ribbons on occasions, and copper bands, the bells and various ornaments. Some of the horses in hot weather wore little straw hats perched gaily upon their heads, with ribbons and even a flower in the hatband. Ours

too had to be in the fashion, to carry a pointed straw hat between the ears like a little circus horse. There was a good reason for this fashion, for the hat kept the blazing sun from the head and it attracted flies away from the horse's eyes. The pony seemed proud of his ornamental head-dress, he tossed his head while people stared and smiled. Horses' ears were sometimes enclosed in netted ear-caps, in scarlet or blue with white tassels like miniature night-caps, and again this was to prevent flies from bothering the animals.

The railway vans always had fine well-groomed horses with

polished brass and netted ear caps, which we all admired. The railways were rich, and could afford the best for their animals. The father of a school friend was the buyer of hay for the railway horses, and he travelled first-class on his journeys when everyone else travelled third in our slow trains. This showed the importance of the horses, we thought.

The railway 'drays' had heavy horses with great feet, feathered with masses of hair which was combed out and flowing, and the manes were thick and long, sometimes plaited. A stout, elderly man with a goitre on his neck used to drive the dray, with heavy bales of cotton for the mill in the valley. The dray went slowly along the road, at walking pace, and the man nodded on his high seat, half-asleep, perched above his load, holding the reins lightly, his eyes half shut, for the horse knew the way. The river sang, the birds flew across from hedge to the water, and the dray bumped over the rough stony road, acting almost with the precision of the steam roller. Every day he went by this long winding bottom road, our turnpike, with its white layers of dust which rose up and enveloped him until he looked like a miller. Of course the water-cart never came away from the little town and the roads and villages were left in their inches of velvety dust.

We cantered past him, and he raised his whip in acknowledgement of our salute. Sometimes we saw him stop at a water-trough to give his horse a drink. His horse brasses shone, they were strung right down the front, on martingale and on the horse's great head, a series of suns and moons and devices, with bells ringing on the leather strap. He was an institution, a traveller as regular as clockwork, and as slow as an ancient pendulum wagging through the hours of winter and summer. His goitre was wrapped in a thick scarf, he sat humped in the shape of one of his own bales of cotton, drawing into the hedge when a trap or cart came hurtling along, then resuming his own unhurried pace, the figure of old Time himself.

There was a game children played, with three children abreast as horses, arms linked together behind their backs, and a child to drive them. A string caught the outside arms of the horses, to make reins for the coachman. They ran with high-stepping action, they pranced and cavorted, while they sang a gay little rhyme.

> *Bell-horses, bell-horses, what time of day?*
> *One o'clock, two o'clock, three and away.*
> *Master is coming and what will he say?*
> *' Bell-horses, bell-horses, here is some hay.'*

We could tell the time of day by the great dray which met certain trains and came along the valley from the goods yard, with its tinkling horse-bells.

In the small town we saw the travelling tinker with his hand-cart, and ornaments of brass. He mended kettles and pans, he sharpened knives and recaned chairs. As he seldom visited the villages over the hills, and he never came to us, he was a romantic person, a traveller from some unknown fabled town who wandered the roads, keeping to the populous places. We sat watching the little stone wheel spin round like our big grindle-stone, as he sharpened knives as swiftly as our knives were ground. His movements were quick and spry, he was a lively dark-eyed man, a gypsy-looking foreigner.

Often we saw a dog-cart, of golden yellow, with high wheels which spun round at a dizzy rate and flashed in the sun like diamonds. The horse had no blinkers, and his eyes gleamed and turned back to show the whites, his heels kicked, he tossed his head and pranced and backed, to show what he could do. He was a nervous arrogant creature, and the coachman held him tightly, with never a glance around. By his side sat an elderly lady whom we knew very well, for she was the niece of Florence Nightingale, and we bowed and smiled and felt happier when we saw her there, with the groom sitting on the back seat, his arms folded, his body taut, ready to spring down and hold the horse's head.

Next came an open landau, and again we knew all about it for it was the carriage that came from the little hotel to meet all trains at the town station. It cost sixpence to ride in it, and very occasionally we had the pleasure of sitting, with our buttoned best boots resting on a fur rug, which was bliss indeed, and our bodies on the slippery leather seat, while we leaned back in luxury and looked to left and to right, hoping that somebody whom we knew would see us. It took us as far as the fish-pond and then we had to alight and walk the rest of the way home, through the rocky defile, and along the roads, over the river, and away to the open country.

There were many bicycles, and one penny-farthing, which was ridden by a terrifying man, who always alarmed us, with his fierce gaze and his red tie. Bicycles went on the footpaths, and when we were walking they nearly knocked us down, for there was no causeway on the long winding road. In the town they had to behave but on the country lanes they had their own way, and I climbed on the wall when one came ringing its bell towards me.

There were wagonettes of people, who had come to see the sights in summer, and brakes with a cricketing team, and market carts, and milk floats, and covered wagons with paraffin barrels and tun-dish at the back, and pots and pans and brushes hanging from the centre beam which went from the front to the rear of the little cart. The tarpaulin was rolled up like a tent, so that the goods could be seen, but when it rained down came the cloth and covered everything. This was one of the special carts, which we admired, and we always wished to stop and stare, but on we drove, out of the little town, to our own less populous roads.

There we saw a grey donkey with a little girl riding and a governess walking by its side. We drew up, and our pony stopped while we leaned down and talked to the governess. Sometimes the donkey came up the hill and the child visited us and drank milk, silent and aloof and shy. We patted the donkey, but we felt it belonged to another world, a stiff starched world, unseeing and proud and rich.

The carriage from the Castle came along the road, with

liveried coachman wearing a cockaded hat, and the groom by his side, and the squire's wife sitting in state without the friend-liness of the lady in the dog-cart. They whirled past, with flash-ing wheels, and left us far behind, humble and lowly, as we drove on the white dusty road between the hedges full of roses and honeysuckle with the river singing beside us. The travellers were like our skipping rhyme—when we sang, 'Coach, car-riage, wheelbarrow, cart', and danced in and out of the turning

rope. 'Rich man, poor man, beggarman, thief,' they went along the country roads.

So the travelling carts went on, and occasionally we saw vehicles from earlier generations, carts which had survived the changes of fashion, because they were drawn by horses, and horses were always beautiful, and always in demand.

I was lately reminded of some of these by a sheet of news-paper which I found in the lining of a drawer of my writing desk. It was the notice of a sale on the 1st of June, 1827.

Lot 1: A comfortable Family Gig, with lamps and harness in good repair.

Lot 2: Neat two-wheeled Caravan (will carry six), fitted up with Cushions, Curtains, Glass and Venetian blinds, with a Dickey in Front.

Lot 3: A light Market Cart, with a Cover. May be seen at the Raven Hotel Yard, Shrewsbury.

❦ V ❦

Boggarts and Sprites

There are some experiences, tenuous as a shade, which seem to rekindle old primitive fears and superstitions, and to bring to life something long forgotten. Ancient memories are awakened, from centuries long past. These terrors have no real foundation, unless they have come out of the dim ages when man was alert and sensitive to every shade and feeling of nature. The expression used in the North of England for a sudden fright is 'Her took boggart,' and a boggart is an entity of the imagination, a fearful one, tall and terrible, the personification of darkness. These fears came from the slightest stimuli, a shadow, a movement. They arose from a perception of the unseen, which children share with horses and dogs. They were intangible, and we couldn't describe the fears. Beneficent beings, guardian angels, who shielded us from harm, malevolent ones who sought to destroy us, they were all there, they came out of nothing and to nothing they returned. They dwelt in the ether, disembodied, and they took shape so that they were visible. Then, their business done, back they drifted like smoke, to the unseen. I knew a Boggarty man, a Boggart house, and a Boggart Lane, a joke in the day, but eerie at night.

We carried candles as we walked about the house, bearing them from room to room, across the dark hall, shading them with our hands from the sudden draughts which sent the small yellow flame 'swaling', swinging high and low, as it floated away from the wind. Long shadows ran up the walls, and curved along the ceilings with shifting uncertain dips and

46

mows; circles of light danced on high, and dark spaces surrounded our feet. This semi-illumination was a source of private joy and secret tribulation to us; it was ever-changing and
magical. Bouquets of light fell on the table, and everything
in the circle of the radiance looked very beautiful, richly
painted with gold and glitter, but beyond in the darkness the
cupboard in the thickness of the wall creaked as if a body were
imprisoned within, and I knew there was an oil-painting of a
man's head, very terrible because it was cut off at the neck, put
away on a mildew-smelling shelf of the lower cupboard. The
musical box suddenly tinkled a tune to itself, as if it had been
touched by a shadowy hand, the bookcase on the wall trembled
with shadows and pointing fingers of light. The heavy gilding
on the wall-paper, where gold leaves hung, caught the candle
flame and seemed to quiver, with flower petals and birds swaying, while the brass of handles and candlesticks made points of
light remarkably like eyes.

I lay awake, once upon a time, night after night, watching an
eye that with baleful glare was fixed upon me. The eye was near
the top of the bedroom door, and I dare not shut my own eyes
lest it should come near. In the daytime it was a brass hook for a
dressing-gown, but by the light of the flickering fire it was a
witch with one eye and a long body. The ice-cold air seeped
through the room in spite of the fire, and the owls hooting in
the trees seemed to be in league with that witch. Nor could we
ever speak of the fears and perils against which we nightly
prayed.

'Lighten our darkness, we beseech thee, O Lord; and by thy
great mercy defend us from all perils and dangers of this night.'
We had knelt down, sometimes on the kitchen floor, sometimes
in the luxury of the bedroom by the fire, and made this prayer,
and still the invisible ones assailed us. We might be frightened,
but we were not afraid.

The house had its secrets, its memories of many years, the
centuries when some kind of dwelling had always stood on
those foundations, and it was aware of us. We were a very

inferior part of it, and it was dominant. Yet, as I recognized this early in life, I too shared its secrets and listened to its talk. Large iron keys to fit no locks, queer old objects whose use had been forgotten even by my father, strange things of wood and stone lay on shelves of barns and hung on the hooks and each one seemed to have a message from that past. One curious ornament, carved from wood, with round head and angular body, stood under the yew trees. Nobody knew its origin, although I thought it was an idol, and I never touched it.

There is a shape of bed-clothes, which can catch the heart and set the pulse beating furiously. The white sheets drawn back in a heap sometimes have an inimical appearance, as if a breath of life would endow them with fearful aspect. They cannot move without that mystic breath, but they wait, and we see their silent waiting. If the spirit came into them, they would arise and wave their white arms, like the figure which appeared in that incomparable ghost story 'Oh whistle and I'll come to you, my lad'. From the window looked out a face of 'crumpled linen', and many a face can the imaginative see in the creased and crumpled sheets.

Shapes of empty clothes lying on chairs are fearfully alive in their own right. They dangle, half-inflated with the late occupant's form, ready to be filled with another shape of air. They wait to dance off, in a witch's jig of air and magic, and I am constrained to flatten them and fold them, and remove the temptation for the airy sprites who may wait for entry.

Clothes hanging up take on a sinister appearance, but garments in wardrobes are captured and enclosed in space, and made very respectable. Our wardrobes were lined with blue and crimson flowered cretonne, and this gave such a comfortable and warm look to the interiors, every article was perfectly safe. My mother's best dresses hung there, turned inside out, with the separate linings and fullness of gathers and frilled skirts. My Sunday frock and second best were there, and tartan cloak. There was a sweet odour of camphor and lavender and lad's

48

love. No fears could enter the wardrobes, for there were doors and locks and keys.

It was the Cinderella everyday clothes on the hanging wooden pegs on the walls that were the source of trouble. Dresses hanging up were like Bluebeard's wives, swinging there. Clothes hung behind curtains were worse. They stuck out sharp elbows, and made pointed projections which disappeared when one tentatively touched them. They squeezed together and whispered in the darkness. They hung with no feet, but sometimes, when a pair of kid boots was placed on the floor under them, away from the dust, they took those boots and attached their filmy bodies to them. Transparent bony legs came down from the skirts and some astral figure stood there, behind the curtain.

Perhaps candlelight and the silence of an old house evoked these apparitions. I am sure no ghosts would enter a pair of trousers dangling from a wooden peg if the vibrant hard electric light blazed from the ceiling. But a candle flickering and blowing out with a breath of nothing at all, requiring a fumble of matches, and the quick spurt of yellow flame, followed by the timid pointed

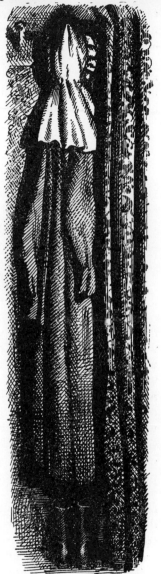

candlelight, was the accompaniment of strange and elusive figments of the imagination which had to be kept secret at all costs.

Sometimes it happened in the blue dusk, when the moon was rising and the first stars pricked the sky. We were out in the hills, blissfully happy with cold air streaming through our blood, and the wind singing high in the trees. Then, a sack

thrown across a hedge took on the appearance of humanity without the warmth and companionship of human beings. It was a ghostly inflated entity, alive as the quick-set hedge upon which it sprawled. Perhaps it drew vitality from the sap of the hawthorn which gave it the power to walk or float along after dark. A sack took power from the earth itself, and many a time we eyed it, shying and backing for a moment, hesitating, then sidling past with 'It's only an old sack', but we were never quite sure. A wandering spirit might find it and dress in the brown hessian, and a sack inflated by a gust of wind was much more of an elemental than any white-sheeted ghost of popular fancy. A ghost would have been welcomed, but a boggart was different. Scarecrows, too, standing alone in the ploughland, scared more than the crows, and I never can pass an old scarecrow in the moonlight without looking behind me.

This aliveness came at the moment of evening when the sun's

long fingers point through the trees and beckon the creatures to come forth. First the dryads run through the leafy woods, to leap and hide among the gilded beech trunks. Everything has its own long shadow—house, haystack and tree. Elongated and distorted they move, brought out by the wizardry of those outstretched hands of the sun. They pursue the wayfarer, and tease him, but they are friendly, for they are intent on their own escape and pleasure.

The moon shadows are more potent, and we thought many inimical things were about. 'A pesky thing, a flitter-by', said the farm man, and he may have meant an owl, or something supernatural. Moonlight, cold and beautiful, cast a fugitive bloom on the fields, like mother-of-pearl, and the cattle lying there in summer were ethereal and of some fairyland. Life was shifted to another plane, more ancient, and a cry of a vixen borne on the still air might be something out of primeval times, and the white wings of an owl, moving noiselessly across, might be a flitter-by or a ghost.

It was a fifth dimensional world, beyond time and space, and, as soon as I stepped out of the kitchen with its warmth and lamplight, its security and kindness, I felt wary and watchful. I shivered, but not with cold or fear, as I saw the milky moonlight lie on the fields spread over the hill to catch every gleam from the sky. The valley was a silver bowl, and we were high up near the rim, and over the edge might lie the mountains of the moon. Murmurings and rustlings and listening were there, for the earth hearkened to the voices. I could hear the song of the river deep at the bottom of the valley, and then the whistle of a train beyond the hills. A vague whispering was all around, and the ancient stones were awake.

Those great blocks of gritstone, weathered to shapes of dragons and beasts, jutted from the earth, in woods and fields, and they had names among us. Far away in the little village churchyards the moonlight was waking old bones, startling the dead and lifting them up to peep at the sky, but these gentle shades were for the tales of the village people, and we only

heard them occasionally, when we sat at tea parties and no one thought we were listening. Our stones were different, their silence was hostile, they were old as the hills, and wise as the Bible. Perhaps we associated them with 'Oh, Baal hear us', or pagan rites, or fairytale. If they had been the stones of Stonehenge they could not have filled us with greater awe and also admiration, but they lay far apart in diverse places, one across the deep valley, another in the field, another in the wood, and others beyond the hill, where a menhir stood erect in a neighbour's meadow.

These ancient stones, whose rough black surfaces were embossed with bright lichens, in gold and tawny discs like old coins, whose cracks were cemented with emerald moss, lay dreaming through the centuries, but at nightfall, under the visiting moon, they awoke and breathed and stirred in their beds of earth, and maybe they moved down to the river to drink, or they rose up like Behemoth and roared at the stars. Who knows what happened?

By moonlight anything could occur. The clothes hanging all night in the orchard drying ground, to bleach with the same powerful moonbeams, stretched their vacant arms, and swung from the steel line which fastened them to the apple trees. Handkerchiefs lay on the grass in the small enclosed lawn, to whiten there safe from the hooves of the wandering horses, to feel the power of the moon's rays. A flash, a flutter and up they might rise like ghosts.

'I'm frit to death', said the servant girl, hurrying in with her eyes wide and startled, her red cheeks glowing as if someone had kissed her. 'There's a mizzling something, wavering and wanting me.'

'Nonsense,' said everyone, but we pondered it. To go upstairs at dusk to a bedroom was an alarming experience, but it had to be done without a tremor, for it was vital that nobody knew one's fears. The room lay deep in silence, a waiting apprehensive stillness. The darkly moulded bed, the round oak table, the Queen Anne table, worm-eaten but beautiful, the chest of drawers and washstand, all must have been conferring together, until that moment, and the glimmering white cross on the bracket which was the emblem of Christianity alarmed the young by its intense snow purity and had no effect on these others. On my entry they instantly held their tongues, impatient for me to go away. Something was going on and I was not

wanted. They waited, watching me in an intent immobility as if frozen. The atmosphere held the feeling of vibrating air, as they fled back to normal on my approach. A second earlier I should have caught them.

I went about my task unhurriedly, perhaps to get a clean handkerchief for my mother, or to turn down a bed, or to light the bedroom fire. As soon as I finished, my eyes taking in every movement around me, as soon as I shut the door they would come and continue their talk.

Continually I faced the unseen perils, never refusing to walk in the darkness, indeed welcoming the combat with the invisible, which I might be allowed to see sometime, for the powers of the unseen world must never know I had any fear.

The film Snow-White revived some of the apprehensions of childhood, and although I sat serenely in my velvet seat in the London cinema, for a few minutes I was a child returning from school through the woods at twilight, with my lantern casting flickering beams on the stony uphill path, and the trees coming out of the shadows to leer at me. Once again they dipped their branches and scratched my face as the wind blew a gale, and I felt the long skinny fingers of beech and oak whip my cheeks, and the sharp tangle of briars and holly scratch my legs as I stumbled into the banks. Stung, lashed and beaten I fought my way against the storms in the darkness, aware that all the forces of nature were abroad and awake. Home was a distant star, shining down, at the world's end, and every living thing there would applaud my safe return.

At night the trees regained their ancient powers, which had been lost when God had chained them by their fibrous roots. At night they shook off their fetters, and rose to their full stature with proud bodies bursting with wild energy, and branching arms uplifted to the sky. The shapes of the trees became human. They quivered and shook and whispered in an unknown tongue which perhaps I might understand if I listened. Perhaps it was Latin, the universal language which I was already learning.

The oaks standing aloof in the fields and hedges became kings, and we had a reverence for them, an admiration and respect. Their voices were old, they roared in the storms, they were filled with scorn, and I walked past the solitary giants, glancing behind to see if they would throw a bough at me. In daylight they were friends, companions, beloved, and only in darkness and in storm were they possessed by powers that made them revert to something inimical and unknown.

The earliest fears of childhood were of wild animals, fabulous bears and wolves and lions. All farm animals were familiar as brothers, and from the days of infancy we ran among horses and cows without a tremor, fetching them up, leading them, decking them with garlands and talking to them. But wolves with long red tongues and sharp teeth came out of the snowy woods on winter nights, snarling and howling around my home. I heard them snuffle under the door where the step was worn, and they thumped and banged with terrifying assaults on the heavy wooden shutters. Would they get in, would they burst our defences? I looked at my mother, expecting to see her face go pale, but she only smiled reassuringly, and I felt intensely happy that I was safe from all the hordes around us.

'The wind's blowing up a storm. Hark how it howls! We must pray for the people out in this and the men at sea', said she gently.

The shutters creaked on their hinges, the great trees groaned while the wind rushed round the exposed wing of the house with shrieks as if it would tear down the walls.

'Hark at the poor souls crying in hell,' said the servant maid. She was reprimanded by my mother who shook her head, but I believed that all the souls of the dead were flying out there, and a pack of wolves was running close to the earth.

The origin of these fears was simple enough. The wolves were relations of Red Riding Hood's wolf, which lived quite near in the beech wood. The bears too lived in the woods, descendants of the bears who ate up the children who mocked Elisha. The lions had escaped from a menagerie, and with them was Samson's lion, and the kindly lion of Androcles, who might be a friend of mine, too, if I took a thorn from its foot.

It needed courage for a child to leave the family circle and go out in the darkness to the water trough for a drink of cold water. Bolts and bars were drawn back, and I stepped out in the pitch blackness of the hills, with my little china cup in my hand, expecting the sudden leap of a wild beast. At the same time, I was fascinated by the beauty of night, and the cold air that swept up to surround me. Water was not kept indoors, for its icy coldness would be spoiled, and everyone fetched it fresh from the spring where it came out of the earth, sweet and pure. Shadowy beasts drank there, too, unicorns and lions and the hart that panted. The music of the running water was a charm for us and for everything invisible and visible.

There was one talisman against wild beasts—light and a guardian angel. Carrying my small lantern, a miniature affair with a pointed shell-like roof and a little glass window and a candle burning within, saying a little prayer aloud, I could face wild beasts, savages, and phantoms and witches. They dispersed when the beam of light fell upon them, they backed away, and left me in a magical circle. Lanterns bobbed about the farmyard, into stables and barns, up and down the outside stone stairs, across the fields, to church and to visit our friends. They were companionable, happy protectors, and I was deeply attached to them and to their powers over the unseen. They were 'The Light of the World', in the picture by Holman Hunt, which I had seen in a magic lantern at church.

The world of legend and old tales, of my grandfather's father, and ancestors in other farms, tales of witches and enchantments held me tightly, and I touched my lantern and brought it out from under the folds of my little cloak, and swung it to dispel the fancies and apparitions, the imaginings of a child.

☙ VI ☙

Evocation of Christmas

The afternoon of Christmas Eve was dedicated to our shopping expedition, when we went on foot to the village to buy the rare and beautiful toys which cost a penny. We walked with our mother, instead of driving, because this was part of the excitement, and the sensation of bliss was prolonged by the anticipation of the shopping with no horse waiting outside in the cold and no driver hurrying us away from all the allurements of the village shop. In our pockets we had each our Christmas shilling, to be spent on as many small things as possible, and even sixpence would buy a great number by careful laying out.

We danced and skipped on the hard frosty road, we stamped on the cat-ice in the hollows, we slid on the glassy cart tracks, and we shouted to make an echo as we went under the railway bridge that spanned river and road. It was imperative that everyone called under that fine bridge, which had ferns hanging from the roof in summer and icicles in winter, for the best echo was there. I called to it only last summer, and it was just the same.

We stopped for a minute on the ancient stone bridge which carried the road over the river further on, and we stood tip-toe by the wall to see if any ice had formed, but the river was always too swift for ice to cover it. The fourteenth century bridge was the division between our countryside and the village, and after passing over it we became decorous, and walked sedately. When we arrived at the village of little stone houses which climbed up the long steep hill we went first to the post office to give in our parcels and letters. We looked eagerly round at the velvet-framed views, and the Christmas cards for last-minute posting. The bell tinkled and more people came into the tiny crowded space, so that we were packed like parcels ourselves. Everyone talked, but we managed to spend a penny or two and to get change for our silver. My brother bought a sheet of transfers with lions and tigers. I proudly chose a penny packet of diminutive notepaper and envelopes, pale blue or pale pink, with a rose or a pansy in the corner, meaning Love or Thoughts in the grown-up Language of Flowers. This was one of the most desirable possessions, to be used for poems and tales and letters that were never posted.

The newspaper shop was two doors away, and the newspaper man had a Christmas display in the parlour upstairs. We always went up that wooden stair to see the toys and to buy jewels of glass and bells of silver from the boxes which lay on mahogany tables and spindly chairs, for the enjoyment of the village.

There were shining silver watches which cost a penny each, and Christmas magic transformed them into real watches that only measured celestial time, that made a minute last as long as an hour, that brought eternity to a second.

They had paper faces, and movable fingers which broke off unless we were careful, and a screw to wind up the works. They hung on silver chains with bars for slipping through a buttonhole. We paid our pence, and bought our watches and immediately we were grown-up. We set them by the clock on the 'Greyhound', and we could alter them to the grandfather-clock-time when we got home. We could control time as we wished, and the fingers always stayed at the hour of happiness. The watches told the time as reliably as the sun that travelled over the frosty sky, and the moon that peered icily through the window by night. We put our watches in our pockets, and then we went on to the next best thing.

Besides these useful and important time-keepers, there were sugar watches, which were more fantastic and less enduring.

They disappeared completely before the Fifth Day of Christmas, when

> *My true love sent to me,*
> *Five gold rings,*
> *Four colly birds,*
> *Three French hens,*
> *Two turtle doves and*
> *A Partridge in a pear-tree.*

Pink and white sugar made these delectable watches, and the sugar chains were so brittle we could eat a link at a time, like Hansel and Gretel who took a sugar tile from the roof and a gingerbread brick from the walls of the witch's cottage.

The silver watches were kept for weeks, and sometimes they lasted until Easter, when dandelion clocks soon came to take their place. We brought them out of our watch-pockets, our sashes and belts, we gazed earnestly at them, we moved the fingers with tentative touch, as we heard the clock strike. The sugar watches had only a short life, but a brilliant one.

They appeared in our Christmas stockings, they hung on the Christmas tree, they dangled by their square-linked chains, with their faces turned outward, for, like the moon, their reverse side was never visible. We did not attempt to keep time with them, for even to hold them was a temptation to nibble the edges.

The sugar watches came out of a tray of enchantment, such as only the newspaper man could produce. A half-penny each, all spun from gossamer sugar in pink and white, the trifles lay for our choosing. There were lighthouses, the only kind of lighthouse we had ever seen, although we had heard stories of the Eddystone from my mother. A lighthouse was a very romantic building, and these sugar models were tall and narrow, with green and red lights in the openwork sugar windows, and a picture of a lighthouse pasted in the front. When we held them to the fire, a lamp seemed to burn within the frail structure. They belonged to a world where;

> *I saw three ships come sailing in,*
> *On Christmas Day, on Christmas Day,*
> *I saw three ships come sailing in,*
> *On Christmas Day in the morning.*

There were little flat churches, with towers and red paper windows and porches, and we had no doubt that some kind of service was going on within them for on the scraps pasted over the walls were children in red and blue hastening through the snow to the doors.

There were sugar bells and sugar houses, and sugar castles with pink curling edges to the battlements. There were trumpets and drums and fiddles, each with a small picture attached lest we should not understand the message of fairyland they conveyed. We chose one or two from the medley of pretty objects, and my mother watched us and secretly made her own choice, although we were perfectly unconscious of this, and we wondered at the power of Father Christmas who put them in our stockings.

All these sugar toys gave an air of unreality and magic by their fragility, and of gaiety by the painted scraps which later on, when the ornaments were eaten, would fill a corner of our scrap books.

They had a foreign air, and we were told they came from Germany where the bears lived in the forests and the Brothers Grimm wrote their fairy tales, or from Switzerland where there was eternal snow on the mountains and edelweiss and chamois on the slopes. They were the pure essence of fairyland. It seemed impossible that such delicate objects could be made by human fingers. Only people who had supernatural powers could construct these sugary toys.

In the shop window, standing on strips of white cotton wool simulating snow, were homely animals, pink sugar mice and pink pigs with curly tails of string, stout and familiar and satisfying in their sugar content. Their noses were pointed, their ears were pricked, all ready to be nibbled. They would doubtless appear in our stockings, but again we never noticed my mother's whispered conversations about them.

The newspaper man showed us a set of lead spoons fit for a doll, with a fringed napkin and knife and fork with embossed handles. The leaden blade of the knife would only cut butter, the spoons were the correct size for a dip into a basket of lemon-kali. They were irresistible, and we always wanted them to hang on the tree.

A doll's cup, also made of lead, was elegant in shape, with curving handle and narrow base. There was a teapot, slender and tall, and some plates, all set in a box for sixpence. They were arranged in a cardboard background, which set off their silver lustre and leaden charm, for lead was a metal that interested us extremely. It was mined in the ancient lead-workings of the hills, and we saw the pigs of lead carried in carts from the cupellows where they were smelted, to the canal boats where they were taken to some unknown destination. Lead was our own metal; it made our pipes for water, it made some of our kitchen spoons, and a garden ornament, and dishes. We could see the veins of shining metal in the stones of the rockery. So we welcomed the little lead cups and saucers, and much preferred them to china. We whispered to our mother, and she nodded and bought them, for she shared our love for small toys.

There were little boxes of chocolates, which held about eight tiny round creams not much bigger than peas, or a ring of plain chocolate drops. The lids had pictures of snow scenes, of hayfields, of animals over which we pored as if we were looking at picture books. The threepenny boxes were circular, the fourpenny boxes were oblong, and it was difficult to choose between them, when all were so charming. They were an attractive part of the tree's decoration, and the boxes when empty would hold jewellery from crackers, or treasures of seeds and dried flowers throughout the year.

Besides these toys and small presents, there were the more spectacular beauties of glass ornaments that came out of the Christmas drawer and were added to each year by new ones from the village shop. The obliging newspaper man opened one box after another and displayed his treasures at sixpence a dozen. He limped up and down, always in pain from a shrunken leg, but I thought he had an existence at Christmas next to an angel from heaven. He said the word, and all the beauties of Aladdin's Cave were spread out for us to see. 'Sesame', he whispered, and behold a cardboard box filled with silver, rose and sapphire bells with glass clappers which tinkled like a fairy's bell. Glass balls of gold and silver were there for the tree, and we fastened them to the garlands of ivy and yew which adorned the summits of high clocks and cupboards. Once we had a house of silver glass with red windows, which came from the market town, a silver bird with a spun glass tail to sing on the tree, and an angel with a star. These were breath-taking ornaments which winked in the candlelight, and carried minute reflections of the room in their rounded surfaces.

Candles had to be bought, small fluted candles for the little tree. They burned in hexagonal glass-sided lanterns whose red and green sides could be removed and washed. They hung on the outstretched branches, but their glow was warm and soft in the darkness of the room. Before the house candles were lighted they had a jewel-like effect of rubies and emerald, for coloured glass was something we secretly admired, whether in a door, or a window, a lamp or a lantern. These little lanterns were bought one memorable Christmas from the village shop, and they were used for many years. We had no method of lighting the tree, and there was always the fear of fire in an isolated house.

The Chinese lanterns that appeared each Christmas from the sacred locked drawer in the dining-room made a festival in the kitchen. They had been there before we were born, and my first memories were of these wavering lights swinging under the ceiling in their soft flower-like colours. Occasionally a new one was bought to replace a casualty when the north wind entered and set a lantern alight. We made our choice, hesitating between peonies and Chinese people, wide scenes of river and kite-flying. They were circular and cylindrical, and they waved with every breath of wind that came through the doors with the milking-cans. That they had originated in China was a sufficient reason for admiration, and their concertina folds which allowed them to be packed flat as a penny, their delicate and elusive paintings, the rice-paper transparency lighted by the candles within, gave a poetical feeling, a dreamlike air of unreality and wonder to the children who stared up at them.

They were suspended on the clothes-line which passed through great hooks in the ceiling, and each night until after

New Year they were lighted at dusk before the big lamp. We gazed at them in delight, and watched the fanciful pictures swing in the firelight, and the yellow circles move on the ceiling above.

This lighting of the lanterns was a Christmas ritual, something inherited from the past. It was before the days of the

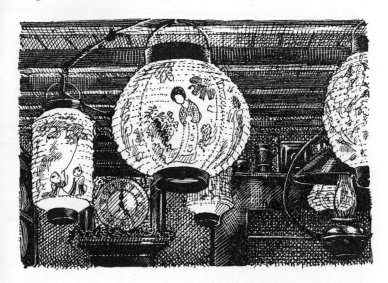

Christmas tree, and perhaps it was part of the old Kissing Bunch tradition, to give the illumination that the globe of holly, apples, and oranges lacked.

The last purchase at the newspaper shop was a sheet of scraps, a Christmas joy chosen from a box of brightly-coloured sheets of many diminutive pictures joined by white bars, so that they could be easily torn apart. There was a page of brilliant flowers, forget-me-nots, roses, lilies, slightly embossed, each with its meaning in the Language of Flowers. A page of scenes of childhood enthralled us, with children in full dresses and long drawers skipping, bird's-nesting, going to school, each painted in the vivid colours of a German print. There were pictures of toys and musical instruments, such as we had never seen, the possessions of rich children, but when we had the pictures we felt we had the reality. The scraps were enclosed in letters, they were pasted on Christmas cards and envelopes, and they made Valentines. They filled the little spaces in the scrap-books, and they made birthday presents. We could only afford one sheet, and the choice was difficult to make.

When we had finished we went out to the blue dusk of the market-place, to the misty air that filled the village square. At the druggist's we bought a flat bottle of smelling salts for three-pence, and a tiny bottle of scent for the same price. These were safe presents for grown-up people, and my mother helped us to pay for them.

We lighted the lantern and started home, my mother walking fast, we running with skips and joyful steps. In the sky shone Orion the Hunter with his jewelled belt, and all the stars were very bright in the darkness of the listening waiting world. We crossed the glittering, talking river, and hastened under the bare trees by the side of the water. It was remote and pagan at Christmas, singing a song of its own, no hymn or carol. When we turned a corner of the road we could see the dark woods, and the lamp like a star from the house, high up above the tops of the trees. The warmth of our hearts almost burned our bodies with happiness and excitement, as we climbed the hill with our parcels. It was Christmas Eve, and angels were about in the sky. Up there they were preparing for the journey to earth, to bring peace and goodwill.

After tea we decorated the Christmas tree. It was a little fir tree from the plantation in the fields where once a great beech wood had flourished. The wood had been replanted with oak and beech, and the small firs grew between to shelter the deciduous trees and keep them warm in winter. So it was necessary to replace each tree in its original place when its work was done. The chosen fir was carried to the barn with the roots intact, and we did not see it until it was brought to the dining-room for decoration.

From the locked drawer of the tall-boy came all the treasure of past seasons, and with them we put our new store. There were baskets we kept from year to year. Some were miniature hampers of brown wicker, hand-made and sturdy. Their lids were fastened with a peg, and they hung by their handles. They were replicas of our country hampers which we sent to relations with apples and walnuts, a half cheese, holly and ivy, a piece of bacon or ham, a rabbit and mincepies. We saw many hampers on the station platform at Christmas, packed to the brim with good food, with feathers and fur showing through the lids, and holly berries shining. There were hampers for the Castle, for the vicarage, for the brewer, for the important people in all the villages, and sometimes a hamper came for us.

The little hampers on the Christmas tree were filled with goodies, with home-made Everton toffee, and nut toffee, with mint rock and the biscuits shaped like walnuts and dice, from the grocer's box. Everyone had a basket from the tree.

Sometimes a pincushion hung there, a flat cushion the size of a penny, covered with silk from the patchwork bag. Or there was a needlecase of flannel, and a black cloth penwiper. Gold paint made many small gifts at which we had been working for weeks. The gilded walnuts with their surprise of a penny thimble, or comfits, or a penny wedding ring, were our chief stock-in-trade. We had a supply of these, made into boxes or pincushions or ships.

Silver frost lay on the flat branches of the fir, and silver icicles hung down, and we even brought in real icicles and snow for the decoration, when we stepped back to admire.

This growing green tree with its glittering array of simple toys and candles and crude ornaments was something so much out of the world, it filled our dreams. Although we helped to decorate it and we had seen the toys in the village shop and made the gifts, we felt it was a creation of God, belonging to a realm outside time. It was something from eternity that had coincided with our own life and age.

It had the fascination of the moon on a frosty night when all the woods were alive with beings, and the fox was barking in the plantation, and the owls calling from the fir trees. It had the enchantment of a fairy tale read aloud by the fire when the shutters were fastened by their iron latchets, and the doors were locked to keep out robbers, and all the animals were asleep in stable and cowhouse and kennel. It had the wonder of Church on Christmas morning, when the altar was decked with flowers, and the pulpit and chancel were gleaming with holly berries, when the scented people from the Castle house-party sat in their pews with a couple of rows of servants behind, and the tumbling, rushing clear river ran outside the walls of the little church, singing as loudly as the choir, while the trout waved their bodies in the transparent water.

It was through the Castle that the rumour of a Christmas tree had come, and the tale was passed from one to another, that a grand tree stood in the Castle hall, filled with candles and presents. It carried parcels and the staff received gifts from its laden boughs. So, in our own small kingdom, we had our first Christmas tree from the woods.

There had always been a Kissing Bunch, which was the ancient way of bringing magic and beauty to a house, and the round glittering bunch of finely berried holly with its flags, rosy apples and yellow oranges, was discovered on Christmas morning when we came down to breakfast, carrying our stockings and parcels. It was conjured up in the night, shining more brightly that its rival Christmas tree, because it hung in the farm kitchen, where all life was lived, where the fire blazed and brass and copper flashed reflections, and snow and frost entered with wind and rain and pools of water, and smell of woods and fields and animals.

There was something primitive and pagan about the Kissing Bunch. Its origin was unknown. The red-cheeked apples, that hung in the holly, the oranges that grew there, the stiff flags of many countries and clowns, belonged to old days, when guisers came to every farm to ask riddles and to sing songs. The Kissing Bunch was for kissing, and we embraced under the magical globe, for kisses were due from any who lingered near the sacred bunch.

Christmas, and snow on the ground in the hills, snow on the fir trees, on barns and stable, and snow on the rough wild unmade roads! Nobody knocks on the door, for it is flung open to the stranger, whose approach is heralded by barking dogs. All are welcomed at Christmas time.

On Christmas Eve, an old man chanted 'The Mistletoe Bough', and we always asked for this ballad, told by the fire while the elders sipped a posset.

> *The mistletoe hung in the castle hall,*
> *The holly branch shone on the old oak wall,*
> *And the baron's retainers were blithe and gay*
> *And keeping their Christmas holiday.*
> *The baron beheld with a father's pride*
> *His beautiful child, young Lovell's bride.*

My mother recited her Christmas Eve poem:

> *'Twas the night before Christmas when all through the house,*
> *Not a creature was stirring, not even a mouse;*
> *The stockings were hung by the chimney with care,*
> *In hopes that Saint Nicholas soon would be there.*

My father asked riddles, and our favourite was:

Evocation of Christmas

There was a thing was three weeks old
When Adam was no more.
This thing it was but four weeks old
When Adam was four score.

This appears in 'Love's Labour's Lost'.
Dull asks:

You two are book-men, can you tell me by your wit
What was a month old at Cain's birth, that's not
five weeks old as yet?

Holofernes answers him:

The moon was a month old when Adam was no more,
And raught not to five weeks when he came to five-score.

The chapter of the Nativity was read to us, and we knelt
down on the stone floor and said our Christmas Eve prayers.
Then we went upstairs to the firelit bedrooms. The waits were
coming to sing carols in the yard. The angels were in the sky.
The shepherds were on the hills. Christmas Day was very near.
We hung up our stockings and wound up our 'silver' watches,
and fell asleep.

❦ VII ❧

The Herb Garden

'Having showed you all the herbes that are most usually planted in Kitchen Gardens for ordinary uses, let me also add a few other that are also noursed up by many in their Gardens, to preserve health, and helpe cure such small diseases as are often within the compasse of the Gentlewomans skils, who, to helpe their owne family, and their poor neighbours that are farre remote from Physitions and Chirurgions, take much paines both to doe good unto them and to plante those herbes that are conducing to their desires.'

So says Parkinson and his words were not forgotten. When we were unhappy and the injustice of the world was too much for us, we retired to the herb garden, a secret corner cut off from the kitchen garden by a narrow flagged path. There, on the damp mossy seat in the ferns, screened from view by a bower of old-fashioned single roses, among ancient bushes of sage, wormwood, rue and the rest of the aromatic company, we recovered our health, good humour and sanity. The sharp medicinal smell of that little patch of herbs seemed to cure all ills, and we dried our eyes and turned our attention to the plants. We pinched with finger and thumb the leaves of pennyroyal, (called Pennyrile by the ancients), the yellow flowers of lace-leaved rue, the beaded sprays of wormwood, the feathers of fennel, the tassels of tarragon, forgetting our troubles in the varied odours of leaf and flower.

Between the cracks of stone at our feet grew lemon-green tufts of camomile with its fragrant daisy heads, and furry musk, sweet scented in those days, and miniature thyme, and white

71

violets. The whole of the herb garden was rich-smelling and evocative of other centuries and earlier generations who had once made their medicines and cures from the herbs growing there in abandon.

On the broad stone walls and low stone-covered roofs of outbuildings the houseleek flourished, and the tall speckled spires of the flowers were raised against the blue sky for our delight in their colour. They had been planted for ointments which my grandmother made for her large family. The thick juicy leaves were pounded and the juices mixed with farmhouse cream to make a salve for erysipelas. They were boiled in milk to allay fevers and to ease headaches. They were mixed with honey for sore throats.

The lovely stiff rosettes had another use. For they were supposed to protect the roof from lightning. As the moisture loving plant retains water, there may have been some justification for the superstition, which was held in many countries, especially in Holland.

On the dairy bench stood stoneware jugs of herbal brews, for everyone sipped these teas made by my mother for our health. Rue tea, a bitter medicine, was an infusion from the green-blue delicate leaves of the bush of rue, which grew to a considerable size in the herb patch. Every morning for a week in spring we had to drink a half cup of this rue tea, to clear the blood and improve the appetite. The medicine cup was small, but we drank with wry faces and many protests, although we had faith that it would do us good. Some people ate the chopped-up leaves of rue between slices of bread and butter as sandwiches, but when I tried this a year ago from my own rue bush I was amazed at the fortitude of the old herbalists who could endure such a harsh repast.

Wormwood tea was even more bitter. The plant has soft grey leaves and flowers like rows of silver beads stitched down the stalks. It grows wild in the south where it is called mug-wort, and I find it every day filling corners by gates, standing high in smoky grey spires which nobody regards, unless the gypsies gather the plant for their own use. I know a lane that is filled with mugwort, and there the gypsies wander, leaving their trail. I always pick a spray to carry with me, to crush in my fingers, for the smell of it, like the old herb-garden, seems to dissipate all sorrows. Bunches of mugwort or wormwood were hung in many a cottage to keep away flies and to sweeten the air.

Horehound grew in the herb garden, for it was used in herb beer, which we made every summer for drinking at hay-time. It was used medicinally, as horehound tea, when boiling water was poured on sprays of the flowers, which are white whorls round the stem. This herb has a reputation for curing chest troubles and bronchitis, coughs and colds. It is sweetened with honey, and in many country places even now the people gather horehound for teas. At the country fairs and at Wakes Week we bought horehound toffee, four ounces a penny. It was made by the stall-holders from horehound juice, liquorice and honey, and an enormous brown heap filled half a stall. We enjoyed the candied sweetmeat on winter nights as we trudged through the snow to church.

Camomile tea was the universal cure for simple ills, and we used so much it was not grown in the herb garden, except when it strayed there, for it spreads like a weed. It grew in the border under the yews. The pale green plants will flourish in arid places, between stones and along dry banks. They have a reputation for reviving sickly plants that grow near them; they are herb-doctors in their own family of flower life.

I wished to have some camomile in my new garden in Buckinghamshire, but I could not buy any at the nurseries and I looked for it in vain in the shops. Then I saw some green tufts growing wild by the side of the dusty road outside the home of G. K. Chesterton. I carried away a few seedlings, which would have been destroyed by the road-cleaners, and in a few months I had camomile springing like a weed from the crannies of the stones and corners of my garden, spreading too quickly all over.

Parkinson, in his book *Paradisi in Sole*, praises the little plant whose daisies are dried for the herbal drinks.

'Camomill is a common herbe well known,' says he, 'and is planted of the rootes in alleyes, in walkes and in bankes to sit on, for that the more it is troden on, and pressed down in dry weather, the closer it groweth, and the better it will thrive.'

However, I find it difficult to walk upon camomile, as the stalks are dry and hard under the foot, unless one wore hobnailed boots. The leaves are crushed but the stalks remain, and one would never think of sitting upon such a spiked cushion.

For camomile tea, half a pint of boiling water was poured on a little bunch of freshly gathered white flowers, and this was infused for about fifteen minutes. Then it was drunk, sweetened with sugar, to make a delicate beverage. In winter dried camomile flowers were used and a tin canister filled with them was kept in the cupboard among the spices.

Fennel, with its bright red berries and fine thin leaves, grew in the herb garden, but it was only used for sauces with fish. I came across it lately in a garden at Eton, where it grew tall and beautiful, a much larger plant than I remembered. Tarragon was a herb used for making tarragon vinegar, and the leaves were chopped and sprinkled in salads. Marjoram, too, grew in the garden, a herb used in cooking.

Balm, whose lemon-scented leaves were gathered for their fragrance, was a favourite herb in many a cottage garden, and I have weeded out roots in different parts of the country, for nothing will deter this plant from spreading. Sprays were added to bouquets of country flowers, and we rubbed the leaves on our hands, for the lemon scent.

Balm tea was a remedy for chest complaints, and for coughs. It was sipped, freshly made and hot. In cooking a leaf or two impart a delicate flavour to fish, especially to coarse fish, and in the war it made many a dull dish palatable.

A sage bush grows in most gardens, whether there is a herb patch or not, and our sage was a little tree with tall spikes of purple flowers where the bees sucked. We were told that where the sage grows strongly, the mistress is the master. It was used for cooking, especially in a kind of savoury batter pudding containing many herbs which we ate with roast pork.

Lemon thyme, golden thyme, variegated thyme, all grew in round bushes along the garden path, not in the herb garden for they were wanted quickly, and the herbs were too far away in their corner. These sweet-scented thymes grew happily in the warm sunny bed, with the enclosing walls for shelter. The cushions they made were so thick and springy one could sit upon them. An infusion with cold water was made, for the usual coughs and colds of country people, and wild thyme from the dry banks of the quarries and hills was as useful as the garden thyme. In these deserted quarries grew eye-bright, a beautiful little flower when it is fully-grown, for it likes a stony ground and some shade. I brought home a bunch of the speck-led white flowers one day from a distant quarry, where it grew among honeysuckle and wild geranium and strawberries. It was hailed with delight as a flower that was once used to clear the eye-sight. Milton mentions this flower in *Paradise Lost*, when Adam's eyes were touched with the herb Euphrasie, eye-bright.

A good part of our herb garden was taken up with green mints of which there were several varieties—horse-mint with its thicker leaves and a strong scent, peppermint and spearmint. They were used for sauces and for mint tea. Lime flowers made a delicious tea, but our own limes were so far away and the branches of the trees so high we seldom used the flowers. We bought dried lime flowers and made the tea, which was sweetened and sipped at night for sleeplessness. Lime flower tea is one of the most popular herbal tisanes in France, and one remembers Proust's evocation of things past, from the taste of a madeleine dipped in a cup of lime-flower tea—the little dried lime flowers in the packet from the chemist's shop.

Some of the herbs that might have been in the herb garden grew wild, and there was one little croft which had so many herbs that perhaps they had once been planted there to make a natural herb-garden. Marshmallow grew on the borders of the croft, and on the high banks, in rosy profusion. Once when I was playing among the silky flowers I was told that the mallow was a herb and it was encouraged to grow near the house ready for ailments. Horses never ate it, and it spread and held up the pink petals and the twisted buds that always attracted us. The seed vessels were our cheeses, which we gathered for our games, and the flowers were unrolled and examined, for they were like furled umbrellas.

A decoction of the flower stalks and leaves was used for sore throats, once upon a time, and country herbalists still make it. Betony was used for many cures for it was supposed to be the best of wild herbs.

Yarrow grew down the banks of this croft, another herb with a tradition of healing. Its fragrant flowers and leaves are unnoticed, but they have a strong rich smell when one touches them. In Buckinghamshire by the roads the heavy pink, lavender and cream panicles of flowers decorate the way. It is a flower that likes company, and hates loneliness. Wild garlic was a well-known pot herb, for those who could endure it.

Plantain too, called waybread, was famous for its cures, and in Cheshire and Lancashire it is still gathered for plantain tea, and for healing wounds. Wild comfrey grew among the rocks, and we admired the large plant for its luxuriant growth, and bells like ivory thimbles. It had been preserved there for healing. Wherever I see it, whether by the side of the Thames in the water meadows, or on a common, it always seems to carry a distinctive air, an importance, as if it had once been treasured not only for its use but for its individuality.

Tansy grew in the pastures, in odd corners, where there was a little shade, and this was a wild herb that had once been much used. It had a corner in the herb garden, but it was really an intruder. Tansy tea was made from the flat buttons of flowers which are the colour of old gold. Bunches of tansy which we picked for the pleasure of the heady rich smell, were suspended to perfume outside chambers and storerooms. It was used to

make a hair-wash for very fair golden hair. Tansy pudding was once eaten in Lent, as a bitter-sweet addition to the diet. Gammon of bacon, with tansy pudding, was the old country dish.

Borage too was wild, and I have found it in many a garden where its use has been forgotten, and in hedgerows, where its forget-me-not blue flower shines out. The flowers are pretty

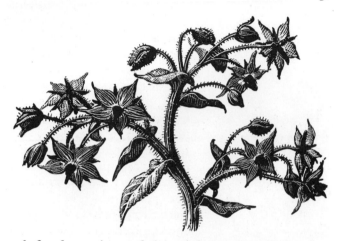

enough for decoration and the petals can be added to a salad. The leaves are put in claret-cup or any drink, for they have the property of cooling the liquid as with ice.

Some herbs in the little herb garden were used for their perfume—rosemary, lavender, lad's love and lady's love, woodruff, which we called new-mown hay, and scented geranium. We could not grow the bay, but in Cheshire I had a fine tree, which was grown from a cutting. From this tree I brought new cuttings south, but the bay trees do not flourish and my trees are only small bushes, which never get any larger.

Parkinson has an admiration for the bay.

'It serveth to adorn the house of God as well as of man: to procure warmth, comfort and strength in the limnes of men and women by bathing and annoyntings outward, and by drinks inward to the stomacke, and other parts: to season vessels etc., wherein are preserved our meates, as well as our drinkes: to crowne or encircle us with a garlande, the heads of the living, and to sticke and decke forth the bodies of the dead, so that from the cradle to the grave we have still use of it, we have still neede of it.'

Lad's love and lady's love grew in every garden, and scented geranium flowered in every cottage window. Sprigs of the

leaves were gathered to add to bouquets, with the lad's love for company. Rosemary has lavender blue flowers, which come out early in April on a hot sunny sheltered bank, but in other parts of the garden it is a month later and the flowers are a paler blue. We use rosemary to keep moths from the clothes, and to sweeten the linen.

Recently I saw a very small neat herb garden which was most attractively arranged on the lawn of a Buckinghamshire Tudor cottage. The little herb garden was circular, contained by old red brick, in divisions round a small dovecot.

Each segment contained a different herb, so that although there was room for each to spread, it was confined within its own brick border. Tarragon, bergamot, sweet cicely, several mints including peppermint were there, with rue, horehound, wormwood, thymes of various scents and marjoram. The garden was like a clock with herbs pointing out the hours, a delightful container of scents and medicines.

VIII

Weather Report

The livelihood of the countryman is dependent on the weather whose moods he studies and consults, whose vagaries are his despair. His background is the earth itself, the seasons, the sun, the changing moon, so it is not surprising that many of the sayings and superstitions of the country-bred man are connected with weather lore, handed down to him, remembered while the B.B.C. gives out its weather report. There is a perpetual viewing of the sky, a humanity is given to the weather, a personality is projected there as the wind buffets and roars, and cracks its whip to make the leaves dance, the rain spits, and the sun smiles and caresses the fields.

Will it be a dry year? Will it be a wet season? The questions were asked with curiosity of the weather prophets, those diviners who sat in the market-place, or at their doors, scanning the skies with acute observation, and we balanced one answer against another, with an element of disbelief, for no man has yet attained the art of divination of the future.

A drought meant small crops and scanty grass on our hills, with less milk and a poor harvest, with hay to buy the following winter to eke out the stacks. It was a time of loss. The ground would crack to expose the rocks, and on the high pastures the turf would be yellow and slippery. Sometimes a spring dried up, but there was always running water, from springs deep in the earth, and the droughts never caused the eternal water to disappear.

Too much rain meant the spoiling of the harvest, with wages to pay, wet or fine, and men waiting disconsolate in the barns.

The grass was beaten down so that the mowing machine could not cut it, and the wet grass spread out to dry could not get enough sun to make it ready for cocking and stacking.

A wet summer was worse than a drought, and the gloom of many days of rain after St Swithin's Day could not be dispersed. We prayed for fine weather in church and at the fireside. We prayed for rain when the sun beat fiercely down and the earth was dried up. There was a feeling of kinship with the people of the Old Testament, who implored heaven for gifts, and privately I used to wonder in times of heavy rain whether the flood had come once more, and we were about to sail off in our Ark.

The sky was scrutinized as if it were an illuminated missal with pictures of angels and rainbows and round-faced cherubs with wide-open mouths blowing for the wind. Its splendour was not missed, for there was always somebody on the watch for events up there. We had an admiration and reverence for the heavens with their fantastic ever-changing clouds by day, their shooting stars by night, and never a night passed without the little gold meteorites rolling like marbles over the sky. They seem to be visible to some people, while others miss them.

We marvelled at the glory of the sunset, at the bands of purple and scarlet that painted the autumn sky, and we stood and watched the changing colours, our only picture gallery, while the old people forecast the weather from the sight.

We went out to see the great clouds threaded with beams of light, called Jacob's Ladder, up which the invisible angels ran to heaven and earth. It was a sign of rain, but a lovely sign held up in the sky. The rainbow, too, called us out, to wonder at the colours, to see the double rainbow, and its inversions and reflections, to repeat the order of the spectrum and compare it with the light through the crystal drops of a chandelier.

There was the great anvil in the thunderous sky, on which the thunderbolts were forged. In childhood they were God's thunderbolts which He might cast down at the wicked, including myself, but later they became the bolts of Jove. We saw a giant blacksmith hammering up there, on that white anvil, cast-

ing down the lightning and the thunder. This anvil is still my
most reliable piece of weather-lore, and I seek it in the sky ever
amazed at its shape and level surface, and the swift coming of
the storm which it heralds.

Yet it was not for beauty alone that the sky was watched, but
for the signs and portents and odd little predictions that came

out of the well of the observer's stored wisdom. It was necessary to know something of the most unpredictable science of
Meteorology, and judgments were balanced against observations.

Many weather proverbs have arisen from the contemplation
of the countryman and they are often quoted with cynical
amusement, as the superstitions of untaught men, but the
proverbs were not accepted blindly, they were based on the
observations of hundreds of years, an oral tradition of weather.
They were the rough and ready rules which had to be supple-
mented by observations of winds and sky. The strength of the
wind, the quarter from which it blew, the way the wind
changed, all were taken into account, as if the men were at sea
with their ship tossing on the waves. The earth was a ship
moving through eternity carrying us with it as passengers. I

could almost see the sailors in the rigging up aloft, for on the hills we were aware of the earth holding us up.

The wind, the clouds, the sun and moon, the habits of animals and flight of birds, all were part of that old weather-lore of country people, which goes back to ancient days.

We watched the deep purple thunder clouds mass over the deserted quarry and wooded hill behind it, when an unearthly emerald light fell on one field, which was singled out, as with a spot-light, by the storm. All work was stopped, as we watched the storm's swift progress. We felt safe, on our rocky island which was part of the earth itself, but we were anxious for the animals. Precautions were taken against lightning, and horses and cows sheltering under an oak tree were driven to an open shed, for there were warnings against oaks in a storm. The prevalence of stricken oaks is a well-known fact, which can be verified.

Indoors during a storm there was a ritual of protection, based on feminine tradition, not always shared by men. A door was left ajar to the full storm, with a window slightly open so that if the lightning entered it could pass through without hindrance, in the draught of air. A visitor once insisted that the bedroom mirrors should be covered, but when we were alone with no frightened friends, the mirrors were left, for we did not believe this. No sewing was done, no scissors were used, no scythes and steel implements were held, and indeed the skies were so black the rooms were almost shrouded in darkness, and everything was left as we watched the play of the lightning around the hills, and counted the seconds between flash and thunder, to discover the distance of the storm's centre.

We had no lightning conductor, although we were high in a stormy area, but the elm tree that hung over the house was said to be a good conductor in itself, and the house was never struck. One night, when I was out in the storm, a large stone trough at the door was cracked and the blocks of stone pavings splintered. Some of the oak trees were caught by lightning, and there was one tree on the horizon, perched on a near hill, that was naked after a storm. We called it 'the stricken tree', and we climbed into its bare branches to gaze over the valleys.

In the hall were the barometers, which hung one on each side of the oak bureau, with the missionary box and the brass candlesticks. One belonged to my father's family, so it had always hung in that spot. The other came from my mother's home, and it was a gentle rival which was seldom noticed. My father's glass was Queen Anne. It was in a long oak case, with a little glass door over the readings at the convex surface of the mercury. The door had a little latchet of brass, which nobody was allowed to touch, and the barometer was set with a minute pointer. There was a gabled turret, and a tiny spire at the top, over which we hung a bunch of holly berries at Christmas.

The second barometer was made of mahogany, a Georgian glass with inlaid wood. It had a round silvery face like a clock, and delicate lacy fingers, which my mother set now and then. It said 'Stormy, Much Rain, Rain, Change, Fair, Set fair, Very dry', but all this chattering information was taken with a grain of salt, for the paternal barometer said nothing at all.

My father took his readings from his ancestral glass. It was read morning and night at the same time each day, and when there was anxiety about the weather the glass was consulted at noon, and the movement added to that of the wind change.

The weatherman high up at the end of the barn was an important sign, and he (for we always spoke of him as a living person), told a great deal. His pointing finger caught every movement of the wind in that exposed place, as he swung there between the points of the compass. A change in the wind's direction was observed at once, and we might have been mariners, with masts plunging through the swift-moving clouds. I watched my father stand on the stone platform of the Master's Chamber, gazing over the valley to catch the feeling of the wind, the signs of rain, the humidity, and all the small portents of high cirrus clouds and great cumulus clouds. He kept an eye on the outstretched arm of the blue man on the roof above, and he watched the flight of birds, the settling of rooks, the move-

ment of cattle, and he listened to the sounds, the distant whistle
of a train as it went into a tunnel, the clearness of voices, but
never a word did he utter of what he saw and thought. So in
every corner of our country men have watched the sky and
made their own proverbs.

The moon gave many a sign, and from her appearance some
details of the country forecasting were made. The moon lying
on her back is the sign of rain. The moon with the old moon in

her arms is the sign of a storm. We looked for a watery moon,
or a moon with the ghostly beauty of a lunar halo and the milky
sky that accompanies this, or a frosty moon. The importance
of the new moon to bring a change of weather has a long tradition behind it shared by all gardeners and country people. When
the new moon appears twice in a month, the weather is bound
to be unsettled is a saying of Derbyshire and Cheshire.

A wheel or ring round the moon is the sign of rain, and the
larger the ring, the nearer the rain.

> *When the wheel is far the storm is n'ar*
> *When the wheel is n'ar the storm is far.*

A large corona round the moon is a sign of fine weather, for
it is made of ice crystals in the higher atmosphere. Moon haloes
and coronae are frequent, but often unobserved, as are shooting

stars and other night phenomena. A lunar rainbow is a sight never to be forgotten, and although it is said to be white, I have seen it with the faint colours of the spectrum.

The backing of the wind was always noted, and with it the smaller signs, upturning of leaves, to show their undersides, the sudden gusts and whirling dust—for this is the sign of a depression, a cyclone. Backing wind, falling barometer, and solar rainbow are the signs of rain.

The strength and speed of the wind was roughly calculated as the blasts swept round the house, or carried straw and sticks in its wild embrace. Later I was interested to discover that the Beaufort scale used by meteorologists in estimating the wind velocity was similar to the rough and ready estimates used by countrymen.

On a near bluff of rocky hill men used once to stand to whistle up the wind, I was told by my father. This was a very ancient custom, and English sailors whistled for a wind in a perfect calm, 'as certain to expect its appearance as a boatswain calculates on the appearance of his crew when he pipes all hands.'

The mackerel sky, the mare's tails, which denote high winds, come from quickly rising and falling barometric pressure.

> *Mackerel sky and mare's tails,*
> *Make tall ships carry low sails.*

> *Rain before seven, fine before eleven,*

was another saying in constant use. Low pressure troughs pass across fairly quickly, roughly in four hours time, and fine weather follows when the glass is rising.

> *Rainbow in the morning is the shepherd's warning,*
> *Rainbow at night is the shepherd's delight.*

To see a rainbow one must be between the arc and the sun. In the evening when the sun is in the west, the shower which makes the rainbow is moving towards the east, the dry quarter, which denotes dry weather to follow. In the morning, when the sun is in the east, the shower moves to the west, which is a wet quarter.

The right quarter, and the wrong quarter,

they said, as they spoke of these directions of wind and rain. When the sun sets with the wind 'agin it', it foretells rain. A dark line round the horizon in the evening means rain the next day, and there was one small portion of the horizon which was always scanned at bedtime.

When as much blue is seen in the sky as will make a pair of Dutch-man's trousers, the weather will clear up.

Children firmly believed this snatch of weather lore, and watched the overcast sky for the small patch which might make the fabulous trousers. Arrangements for picnics and excursions were based by the young on this simple prophecy, but the weather-prophets left it alone.

A small dark cloud, such as the cloud as big as a man's hand which was seen by Elijah's servant, is a sign of rain. A scrap of broken rainbow is a 'weather-gall', meaning rain. A fine day out of season is a 'weather-breeder,' and stormy days follow. A new moon on Saturday is a wet moon.

The green woodpecker is called the 'rainbird' or 'wetile' in Buckinghamshire, and when it calls the weather will be wet. An early spring flock of singing chaffinches is a sign of rain. The common garden beetle was a 'rain-beetle' in many counties, and little boys said that if one killed the creature rain would fall! So many a beetle was spared.

If the 'clock' of the coltsfoot flies away without a wind, rain is coming. The weather will not change while the elder flowers. The old rhyme of the oak and the ash was firmly believed.

The rain on St Swithin's Day was a general catastrophe, and although the forty days was not taken literally, it was thought that a long period of unsettled weather would come which might spoil the hay.

If it rains on Friday, it will rain on Sunday

was a popular tradition, especially with townspeople, but it was not taken very seriously in the country.

The amount of dew on the grass at harvest time was noted, for a heavy dew foretells fine weather, and no dew means rain.

The setting sun was observed, and an angry sunset foretells bad weather. This was of course a different sunset from that in the rhyme:

A red sky at night is the shepherd's delight,
A red sky in the morning is the shepherd's warning.

A warm Christmas foretells a cold Easter, a green Christmas a white Easter. A green Christmas brought a full churchyard.

If it rains much during the twelve days of Christmas, it will be a wet year,

was the old saying.

A prophecy always used on New Year's Day proclaimed

If the sun shines through the apple tree at the new Year, there will be an abundant crop,

and my father always went out to regard the sun through the orchard. Even a glimmer of sunshine pleased him, as it came wavering out of the south.

Candlemas Day, February 2nd, had a crop of weather rhymes, which were confusing as they really belonged to the Old Candlemas Day which was February 14th.

> *If Candlemas Day be dry and fair,*
> *The half of Winter's to come and mair.*
> *If Candlemas Day be wet and foul,*
> *The half of Winter's gone at Youle.*

Again,

> *Where the wind is on Candlemas Day,*
> *There it will stick till the second of May.*

And,

> *If the sun shines before noon at Candlemas, the Winter's not half over.*

> *All the months of the year, curse a fair Februer,*

they said, and we bore with the hard rains that filled the dykes and ditches in February, for the springs were fed and the troughs filled. The month was called 'February fill-dyke'.

March too had its important sayings, and we watched it come in like a lion and go out like a lamb, or the reverse.

> *A peck of March dust is worth a king's ransom,*

was always quoted, to my own bewilderment, but again they said

> *A wet March makes a sad harvest,*

and this was plain enough.

In Buckinghamshire a countryman always warns me of the number of frosts to expect in May. He notes the misty or foggy days in March, and comes along in May with the dates of the frosts. I have been astonished at the number correct.

> *As many mistises in March, so many frosts in May,*

he says.

Another saying about frosts, is

> *Hoar frost and gypsies never stay nine days in one place.*

There are scores of country legends and prophecies of the

weather, and many of them have been found to have scientific reasons for their accuracy. There is poetical feeling and a picturesque and lively imagination in these old country sayings, which are lost in the bare unadorned weather reports we now hear, but the weather traditions are so strong that they will endure in the mind of observant man who listens to the wind's voice and watches the sky.

⚘ IX ⚘

Autumn

Each autumn the invisible ones paint the woods with such splendid colours one cannot even try to remember and to hold them, for it is as though the old gods come out of the earth and mockingly show their powers of transformation to startle us out of our complacency. The Chiltern name for the deep magenta and purple knapweed is a 'paint-brush', and now the colour is splashed in the shadows of the trees, and cobalt shading to indigo is wiped across the horizon. The beeches are flushed with red-gold and amber, the elms which border the fields are pale-washed pure gold, the silver birches lemon yellow, and the cherry orchards and wild cherry trees are like roses.

First a branch here and there is dipped in gold, just a try-out, a specimen of hammered metal, with the veins left green, and we say that autumn is on the way. There is a great beech tree in the wood at my garden's edge, and sometimes the first glimmer of yellow-gold is high, and sometimes it is a bending branch which I can reach. Thirty or forty leaves and no more, and no other tree is touched on that first day of warning. In the woods near there is a bough on one tree, a signal, and again it is solitary. The evening light illuminates this yellow branch, so that it shines like a lamp in the wood. The next day the colour has deepened slightly, the colour has spread over each leaf, but still it remains, the feather of autumn worn in the tree's cap with an air of jauntiness and defiance.

'Just wait and see what I'm going to wear soon,' it says, as it waves its plume and shakes its glittering leaves.

The oaks are dark green, the silver birches have faint gilded edges to their tiny heart-shaped leaves. The elms are unchanged but a wild cherry flames up in a bonfire of red, and the dogwood turns crimson as it catches the sun's evening rays, although it seems dark in the light of day, with no transparency.

One night the moon shines with a strange whiteness. It is much nearer the earth than we imagined. It is a warning moon, ice-cold, with the mountains visible, with the face of the Man-in-the-moon up there. It is no longer part of the sky, but a portion of the earth, watching the fields and woods. That night there is the first frost, and in the morning the grasses are rimmed with minute crystals, which can be wiped off and held for a few seconds of icy coldness. The trees, as they stand in the early sunlight and uneasy mists have gathered something out of the air. They also are nearer, closer to the house, the farm, the village. They are stepping out to meet somebody. The golden branch is red-gold of the dwarf's fabled money, and another branch has turned yellow. The fires of autumn have not yet been lighted, only the little flames are starting, glowing gently, but not spreading.

It is the time of ripe sweet chestnuts which lie in the leaves under the tall twisted trees, like green hedgehogs. We stamp on the husks and break them apart, and take the cream and brown nuts from the silky-lined husk. We shell the nuts, biting off the end to open them, and then we remove the last soft bitter skin, to find the sweetness within. In the great park the fallow deer are watching us as we find the chestnuts, and in the distance we can hear the sudden roar of a buck. Starlings are congregating in immense flocks, covering two or three trees so thickly they look like black fruit. Their wings make a sound like the sea.

Summer is over, and the beauty and exhilaration of the 'back end of the year', is approaching. The gorse bushes are still yellow with their pea flowers, but the almond scent is less rich. Traveller's-joy carries its curling grey feathers, like ostrich plumes for a diminutive hat, the wild roses are brilliant with scarlet hips, sometimes in clusters of a dozen on one straight stem, and the brambles have leaves of the deepest richest green. Soon, as the autumn colours spread, the rose leaves fall, leaving the hips like jewels on the bare spiny branches, the blackberry sprays will curve in semi-circles of crimson and purple leaves, and the maples will turn chrome yellow, while the silver birches flutter their pale gold against the blue frosty sky. Then a flock of long-tailed tits comes twittering and chattering out of no-

where, to dance in the silver birches, and the gold-crests appear one morning in the fir trees whose small cones are splitting and dropping seeds with a distinct explosion.

In the woods, on the hillsides and under the hedges the bracken lies, a web of gold and orange, flecked with yellow, burned to umber. The fronds seem to be made of cork, like one of those Victorian models we saw in childhood, where leaves and stiff flowers were cut by a village craftsman from the corks sent to him by the inn-keeper. Sometimes he made a frame for a picture, or a group of flowers and leaves to be kept under a glass shade, or a miniature church or castle, but always there was an admiring group of people to talk about it.

The texture of the bracken is brittle, the leaves are carved, and the plant is changed to something made by man, a work of art carelessly left by the side of the road, a curving intricate pattern of fronds laid out in a frame to enclose the picture of a green field, or lane. In the western sunshine, the bracken makes a conflagration in the woods. All the hidden colours, the ruddy golds and flames spring to life, and the curling plants give out a golden heat of their own. The bracken is ready for bedding the calves, and for laying down in the rough shelters, to warm the animals.

Once, when I had been ill, I came to the country to a golden autumn, from London. I had forgotten the intensity of the beauty, because I had seen it every year of my life, and it was part of me. I had been unaware of its value. Then I came home, driving at night with the trap lamps shining in the cold frosty air, by the murmuring river, sweeping up the hill to the house with its fires and lights and the good harsh smells of a farm. The scents of the lane in autumn intoxicated me, I was a wild animal returned to its country, as I sniffed at the odours of leaves and moss, of trees and soil, of water and rocks.

The next day I saw the great beech woods, tawny red, clothed in cloth of gold, more beautiful than anything of earth. It was the shock of the beauty that hurt me. I had always seen the colour come so slowly that I had changed with it and accepted it, as summer had turned to autumn within me, but now I had been plunged into the deep richness of full autumn, on a day of perfection, and my senses were stunned.

After that first yellow flag waving in the beech tree the advent of autumn is slow, the change is imperceptible, but the frosts hasten it, the evening air is chill, the days draw in. Gradually the gold spreads through the trees, and new colours come. Apricot, flushed with red, then burning copper, then flame, are the beech trees, when the sun shines through the leaves and makes each tree a distinct flower in the woods.

The hedges of beech, bordering the lanes, are brightly coloured, and the stumps of old trees which have thick coverings of leaves, are autumnal long before the tall trees change their shades. Like the bracken, they colour the earth with tawny gold patchwork, preparing for the final triumph of the great trees in the woods.

The autumn sunsets follow the gold on the woods, and the western sky is layered with crimson bands, rich as the strands of the blackberry leaves. The heavens are as brilliant as the woods, where the cherry is crimson, the beech trees are red-gold and the oaks are bronze and yellow. We stand at the door and gaze

at the west, we hurry across the lawn to the field gate, and try to absorb that deep carmine out of a celestial paint-box, that molten gold, and plum purple, and then we turn for a fleeting moment to look high at the green of the sky. Even as we find the first pricking star, the colour of the sunset has changed, the rose has dropped its petals, and a stormy darkness descends in heavy vapours of black like a drop scene of a gigantic tragedy.

I think with a sudden stab of remembrance of the sunsets of childhood days, when with eyes on the enchanted skies I walked home from school, and then down to the earth I looked and the sun was blotted out by darkness. I hurried on, Red Riding Hood escaped once more from the wolf, and I reached home, with the warm glow of the kitchen fire lighting up the room, sending banners of flames outside.

'Look at the sunset! I've never seen such a sight', they said, and we ran out of the back door to stare across the slopes of the hills and up to that luminous sky. It was our own sunset, our possession, a glory spread out before us, contained in a frame of hills and sky, but our own.

Roast apples in the oven, spilling their creamy sides, sweet chestnuts lying on the oak dresser, fresh walnuts in a heap by the knife-box, a newly-shot rabbit on the floor, cans of foaming milk coming in from the farm buildings, the scents of autumn filled the room with an excitement, as the sunset colours covered the western sky with a promise of eternal beauty.

The air of autumn is sweet and wild, exhilarating and clean. It is crisp as an apple freshly picked from the orchard, and cold as a draught of spring water. It can be deceptively mild, so that one is lured into speaking of an Indian summer, and then it throws a surprise, a flurry of snowflakes, a shower of hail, a wind that blows a hurricane. Out from the oak chests carved with initials and panelled with deep inlaid diamonds, came our autumn clothes. It was exciting to welcome them, and to watch the alterations that had to be made, a tuck to be let down in a winter frock, a hem to disappear, a band of ribbon to lengthen a dress. And then the cloaks, the symbols of autumn and winter!

We always wore cloaks, well-made and elegant in their way, cloaks of russet brown lined with green and blue tartan, cloaks or navy blue lined with scarlet, cloaks of Scottish plaid with a silver buckle. They had hoods attached, and straps to fasten them so that one had wings. Cloaks were made at home when the dressmaker came in the autumn with her paper pattern books, and her thimble, nightdress and slippers. She slept in a little bedroom next to mine, and she sewed very fast all day and evening.

Cloaks never wore out, they never became old-fashioned, but they descended in the scale as the years were heavy on them. Old cloaks were used to throw on one's shoulders on stormy days in the orchard or garden, and a lighted candle or a lantern was sheltered in their generous wraps, as we went outside for drinking water. They covered the sick, who lay on the settle, they were wrapped round little children, they were thrown in the cart among other rugs and coats to meet a traveller. I always wrapped a warm cloak about me when I was driven along the snowy lanes under the stars shivering after a long journey home. That cloak, smelling of stable and herbs and farm, was a welcoming embrace, a country kiss, rough and

warmhearted, a defiance of the winds and weather, as I peered out from its folds up to the sky with more stars than ever I remembered, down to the earth where the trap lamps glittered on walls and banks and hedges. A cloak was used as a blanket for a bed, a cover for a waiting horse, an umbrella in the wild storms when no umbrella could be held up.

In autumn we explored the woods to find berries, nuts, toadstools, and unknown trees. We walked through the drifts of fallen leaves and dragged our feet to make the sound of sea waves. We threw the leaves in showers over our heads, and played games in the deep drifts of gold under the shadows of the woods. Every falling leaf we caught was a lucky day, and we tried to capture the spinning beech leaves as we wandered through the cathedrals of trees.

All-Hallows' Eve came with bobbing for apples in a brown bowl on the kitchen table, and roasting chestnuts, each of which bore the name of a sweetheart. The apparition of a future husband might appear in a mirror as one brushed one's hair by candlelight.

All Saints' Day was solemn with a prayer at night, and the hymn 'Who are these like stars appearing?' The stars always seemed to shine more brilliantly on that night of November.

Then came All Souls' Day, and a great concourse of rooks flew over like the souls of the dead flying for ever. The leaves fluttered slowly from the trees, and as they drifted they too seemed to have a power within them, as if they wished to tell us of some mystery they knew about immortality. All Souls', and the evening sky silver blue, with gold strands of clouds and pink cloudlets, to be swept away by thick masses that cover the heavens in a pall. Miracles happen at All Souls' Day, and the souls of the long dead seem to be moving silently in the air, looking in at the windows, dreaming of their own life once lived on earth.

In Cheshire, the children sang the souling song:

> *A soul, a soul, a soul cake.*
> *Please, good missis, a soul cake.*
> *An apple, a pear, a plum or cherry,*
> *Any good thing to make us all merry.*
> *One for Peter, one for Paul,*
> *One for Him who made us all.*

The cherry trees have waved their pink and crimson flags, and dropped them at last. The silver birches are naked ladies. The rosy spindle leaves have blown away and the pink coral berries are exposed in the hedges, magical wands with rare jewels. The robin sings his autumn song and follows the traveller boldly. The green woodpecker flashes his green wings and laughs for rain. Chaffinches and greenfinches flock together in happy company. At night the owls cry in the beech trees and a full moon looks through the windows. Then a morning of heavy frost, the grass is white with hoar, and the trees are suddenly bare. Winter has come, with winds and snow and rain and a new strange beauty of earth and sky.

X

Choosing a House

Ever since we found houses for ourselves in the woods, where we lived our elysian hours among the trees and rocks in imaginary homes, I have searched for the perfect dwelling-place. It was easy enough in those days, when a spring bubbling up from the grass was the water supply, a hollow in the curving roots of a great beech tree made the larder, and the greensward was the flower-sprinkled carpet of the drawing-room, while a low branch of the tree was sufficient for a bedroom where one could climb and sleep among the leaves.

There was one house I loved more than any other, for it was surrounded by forget-me-nots, an azure mist of woodland flowers. A silver birch made the bedroom, on a higher level in the sloping wood. The house was hidden deep among the trees, in such a lonely place only the poacher, the fox and the badger walked the unseen tracks. Indeed sometimes we missed it ourselves, when we returned with a basket of food for the day, for the house retired among the rocks and became invisible. Great blocks of lichened sandstone sticking abruptly out of the earth made the furniture, a table and chairs. There was even a piano upon which I played to the birds.

The forget-me-nots had decided the house, and they were the chief reason for its habitation. They were a ready-made garden of celestial hue, and we carried nosegays home at the end of the day.

The first real house which I had the felicity of helping to find was the Old Vicarage, where I lived when I was married. It was a whitewashed seventeenth-century house with panelled sitting-rooms, and oak shutters to cover the windows and keep out the cold. There were cupboards in the thickness of the walls, and tiny cupboards over the beds to hold a book and candlestick. The beautiful staircase with newels at each turn, went from the cellars to the big attic, which had once been the council chamber for the town. It was the house where Peter lived in Mrs Gaskell's 'Cranford'.

I was always apprehensive in this charming house, with its many small rooms, and I stepped softly at night with my lighted candle, looking behind me to see who was following. Somebody lived in the cellars, I imagined, and when it was dark they came out and glided up the shallow staircase.

I was aware of warmth and sweetness and good fellowship, but after the shutters had been fastened across the windows, and the candles lighted, the rooms were dim as if no fires or lights could dispel the ghosts who lived there. In the daytime it was gay and bright and lively, for the cobbled streets of the old town echoed with footsteps, with the whistling of boys and the clatter of horses' hooves at 'The Angel'. On May Day there was a May Queen, and the procession moved through the narrow street under my windows. After a year of happiness we had to leave this house and for some years we had no settled home.

At the end of the war we returned to Cheshire, and chose a house in a few minutes, with no hesitation. When I unlocked the door of the ivy-covered early Victorian red brick house, I immediately felt happy. There was an air of welcome in the empty rooms. I pushed open each door, and the place was filled with warmth and goodness. Up the steep stair to the attics I went to see the four rooms with crooked ceilings and tiny windows, and again there was a warmth that had nothing to do with sunshine, for the house faced north-west and was cold.

'Let's buy it', we said at once, forgetting everything. The roof was old, the stairs were many, the garden was small, but the house itself seemed to call us, and in this house we found serenity and peace. I began to write there, in the largest of the attics, with pointed window and beamed ceiling. Afterwards I heard that Mrs Ewing had lived in the house and indeed it had the old-fashioned charm of Mrs Ewing's tales, 'Lob-lie-by-the-fire', and 'Jackanapes'.

A house becomes a living entity, taking on the character of those who live there, absorbing something from them. It has a personality, and an awareness of those who inhabit its rooms. Perhaps it has drawn in the atmosphere of all those who have dwelt in it, and life is saturated in its stones.

There is a sense of adventure in entering an empty house at the precise moment when one steps indoors. One goes carefully, treading softly, listening, intensely aware of the house's own life. I feel myself holding back sometimes, caught in the web of tangled threads drawing me this way and that. Ill at ease I long to escape. This perception of houses is very strong when I enter an ancient house with its character developed and its sense of the past.

The Cheshire house was at last too large for me, but I had a strong tie with it which pulled at my heart. In the little garden grew an apple-tree, very old, with stout gnarled trunk and low boughs where we could climb and sit concealed among the flowers. It was smothered in blossom in spring, the most delicate pink-shell petals of flowers, and in autumn there was always a heavy crop of enormous round apples. They lasted all winter, and I covered the floor of one of the attics with the fruit which we picked in the clothes-basket. I thought I could never leave this tree, but the difficulties of the old-fashioned house at last made me decide to part.

The house I wanted must be small, and easy to work alone, and the garden was more important than the house. I preferred an old house, but I was prepared to take any little house, new or old. I looked at cottages in Devon, Herts, Surrey, Sussex and Buckinghamshire. I found that I was choosing the dwelling for some quite unimportant reason, such as a tree or a flower, a bank of violets or a stream. I nearly bought a cottage because a Pasque flower was blooming by the garden path. The lavender petals were cased in silver fur, and the buds were like a kitten's paws. I was enchanted. I had never seen this flower before, and I dawdled by its side, while the agent unlocked the house and beckoned me to enter. I hurried through the rooms, scarcely noting anything, hastening to get back to those purple flowers in their grey mist of leaves. I asked the name, but the agent did not know. I remembered that it grew wild in the Chiltern hills, and I decided to buy the cottage, but in the meantime the owners changed their minds and I had to abandon my Pasque flower house.

Another house I visited reminded me so strongly of the forget-me-not house of my childhood I could scarcely resist it, but the proximity of crowds of little houses near it embarrassed me even as I stared at the garden paths. The house, which had no feelings at all, had been empty for some months, and forget-me-not and love-in-the-mist had seeded every cranny of the hillside garden. The whole place had gone wild and the flowers spread like weeds. Only the people around me frightened me away, or I should have found myself with a gimcrack little house in a Torquay suburb, and the wireless from every window near.

I nearly bought a little house because a small Christmas tree was growing in the garden. The owners told me it had been their Christmas tree for two years, and I saw it hung with silver bells and golden balls, ringing outdoor and in. I decided I would dig it up and carry it to the wide hall, and cover it with

toys for Christmas, and then I would replant it. The lawn grew close to the windows of this house, and there were no flowers, but the little fir tree was so romantic and shapely in the green lawn I thought I could hear its silver voice.

When a robin flew to this companionable little tree and sang its sweet song, I was captured. The agent smiled, and the owners who were very anxious to sell, talked about the house over a glass of sherry. Then I went back to the hotel and lay all night repenting. It was too lonely. It was suburban. It was a bungalow, and I had never been in one before. I couldn't go upstairs to bed and burglars would walk through the open windows. Even the fir tree would grow big. The next day before breakfast I telephoned to refuse it. There were recriminations and angry expostulations, but at last I was free for I had signed nothing.

After this I was more careful, but the search continued. Always when I entered a house I stood for a while, listening to the breathing of the house, looking for the invisible, receiving impressions of things that had happened, which seemed to come from some source outside ordinary sense perceptions, so that I was perhaps receiving messages of another wave length than those of light and sound. If this was difficult with an agent talking and the householder chattering and showing me the rooms, I visited the house in sleep. I wandered to and fro, about the rooms, opening doors and gazing within. From this nocturnal journey I knew many things and my final decision was made.

Sometimes there was no doubt of the uncanny. There was a lovely house, small, ancient, with a moat around it and a bridge over which we drove. It was fantastically beautiful. It had every virtue. The odd-shaped rooms opened to one another, and little had been changed from pre-Tudor days. The heavy doors swung open of their own accord revealing more rooms, with crooked floors of oak, very homely and familiar to me. They had latches and wooden pins like the cottages of childhood. They were the doors of farm buildings, and as we passed through I expected to see a lamb lying on the hearth, or a calf in a fold, for it must have been a farm once.

The garden within the moat was perfection, an enchanted place of gay flowers and green lawns, which had been tended with such care I felt there was a magical quality about them, and the gardener in the background was in keeping. The flowers were unreal in their size and beauty and variety, they

were illuminated from within, and lilies and roses grew in luxury. The grass was green as an emerald, smooth as silk, and I dare not step on it. I kept to the narrow paths as I wandered round the little timbered Hall with its ancient romantic name.

The agent got tired of my loitering, but I was trying to get the sensation of this old house, I was picking up the threads that hung there for the sensitive to gather knowledge. The house had been empty some time, and there was an intense vitality about it, a whispering, an alertness. I could almost hear it say, 'Here she comes. Shall we have her? Do we like her? Is she for us or against us?'

I wanted to call out 'Is there anybody there?' but I was silent as I listened to many voices.

The agent left me in one of the sitting-rooms, staring at the oak beams of the fireplace, trying to decipher some faint letters once cut there. I was alone, and the heavy door at the foot of the stairs banged after him. I could hear his footsteps as he went up the crooked winding stair to a room above. Then there was silence, but what a silence! Everything was alive, sinister, moving about in the stillness. I listened to the beating of my heart, and in a panic I rushed to the door and ran upstairs with the certainty that a horde of invisible ones was following me. Not for a moment dare I be left alone. The agent calmly talked and I kept close to him, giving no hint of my feelings. Not until we were in the car did I relax. As we drove away I turned round expecting to see a disembodied face peep from one of the ancient windows.

A year later, still searching for a house, I drove with the same man and tentatively asked about the romantic and lovely Hall.

'I thought it would have suited you,' said he. 'An American has bought it.'

I explained that I thought the house was haunted, and he confessed that I was right, but as agent he never mentioned the fact, and the American was not disturbed by any ghost.

I went into Sussex, a county I scarcely knew and there I saw a wooden house, with a gallery which looked down to the hall. It was built in a thicket with rabbits sitting on the doorstep, and foxgloves and willowherb growing close to the walls. I felt that they would enter soon and take back the land that had been stolen from them.

There were few houses vacant but an address was given to me on a bus route. I set out, on a bright spring day, feeling happy for the house had an attractive name. The bus went along a country road so narrow that the hazels swept the windows and primroses grew by the side of the path. I saw myself walking from my cottage, filling baskets of wild flowers.

We passed a house, an ugly villa built on a rise, with firs

and hollies close to its windows and a 'For Sale' notice. I stared with apprehension. It was gloomy and forbidding, a murder might have been committed there, or a future murder might have been planned. I dare not even go to the door.

Instead of returning to the same agent I went to another. He gave me the address of the same house. I demurred, saying that I thought there was something wrong with the place. As he began half-heartedly to deny this, a countryman sitting in the room interrupted.

'It's haunted,' said he. 'That's why nobody will buy it. I know it's haunted.'

He told us that once he was walking home with his dog near midnight. When they came to this house the dog refused to pass. It howled and dragged back. It pulled with such strength he was obliged to leave it and go home alone. The next morning he returned and there lay the dog in the same spot. It followed him, but he could never get it near the place again. Then he heard tales from others, for the house had a bad name. The agent said there might be something in the tales, and we said goodbye.

So my search continued, among houses with dry rot, and houses too large and too small, until one day I was taken to a little house in a neglected garden, but at the garden's end there was a small wood with beech trees. One tree had wide spreading branches and high waving tip. Nobody could feel lonely with such a tree, which had been there long before any houses in the district.

Forget-me-nots grew wild along the paths, cuckoo pint and new-mown-hay grew in the wood, with primroses and daffodils. The house was too near others, but I had scarcely entered it before the agent whispered I must make my choice. I decided at once. There were many disadvantages, but the cuckoo comes each April to pay his first visit to the crest of the beech tree. Green woodpeckers are constant guests on the lawn, and tawny owls live in the wood. The Pasque flower grows in a corner, and the forget-me-nots seed all over the borders.

Such is human longing for perfection, I still desire a little house, with a spring for its water supply, and the curving roots of a beech tree for larder, stones for furniture and a bedroom on a branch where I can sleep and write all day, with no sound but the spring water and bird song.

XI

An Old Account Book

A long narrow vellum-bound book is the account book of the 'Overseers of the Poor', for a small Buckinghamshire parish during the eighteenth century. The church registers go back to 1560, and the details of those buried, christened, and married are given in the parchment registers, in exquisite and minute script. The village account book, which begins in the year 1720, refers to the expenses incurred for parish relief. Even to hold the heavy book is to receive some of the feelings of the past, and when the pages are turned one is taken back in time to the unknown poor people who once lived in this little straggling village on the ridge of the Chilterns, where the church has stood since the thirteenth century. It is a place I know very well, and many names in the register are names that are still common in the village. Woods surround the scattered houses, the farms and cottages, and far away they stretch, blue on the horizon, one layer above another, beech woods with narrow valleys between. The hour-glass of time is turned, the sands fall from one century to another, and the past comes vividly back in the faded brown writing of the parchment pages.

The account book has a grand inscription written within the cover, in elaborate and decorative letters, as befits its importance in the life of the parish. One can imagine the discussions about the wording, the trials of letters, the realization that here was the beginning of an epoch. It is a plain statement of fact, adorned with the trappings of state. 'This Book was Bought in the year 1720. William Plasant and Richard Huthins, Overseers of ye Poor.'

The penmanship is richly ornamental, but clear and legible, with large capitals for the first two words, This Book. The capitals T and B are so highly involved and decorated they must have each taken many hours to design, but there is no sign of hesitation in the scrolls and mazes through which the pen works its way. Convoluted lines spring from the heavy thick strokes of the horizontal bar of the letter T. They fill the cavity of the half moon made by the dipping end of the bar, they curl and twist about the downstroke of the letter, and sweep upwards with

delicate flourishes like the swirling water of a rushing river. Perhaps the wind in the beech trees gave the artist inspiration, or the swaying of corn in the west wind in that high place of the hills, for there is no river, only springs which water the land.

The letter B is even more important, as it is the beginning of the word Book. The two spaces of the letter offer a great opportunity for turning and fluting, for festoons and curls, and the frames of the two halves are filled with the patterns which differ for each part. The twisting lines dip down for several inches, they swing deep on the page, and the date 1720 is inserted in small neat figures in the lower branches of this great initial capital B. Feathers float in the air about the date, like those of a bird of paradise. 1720 is evidently not very important, it is a date in the long chain of the future. The words of the inscription, after the flourishing start, are written boldly, with no decoration, but the final word, Poor, is in diminutive script. as if it were whispered, something to be kept secret in this old account book which is all about the poor.

Below this ornate and fine inscription with its wonderful capitals, is an exercise of penmanship, which is the finale, devised with elegance and beauty, as Queen Elizabeth used to make her looped and intricate design under her signature. It must have been admired and wondered at by all who read the accounts in those early days of the eighteenth century, for the pen seems to have gone through the whole long curving complicated patternmaking without being taken off the paper.

At the foot of the page is an admonition of great importance. 'Remember the Poor.'

This again is ornamental writing, and the capital letter R in Remember is a broad stout letter, much adorned, with ruffs and laces, with ribbons and loops, gay as the Laughing Cavalier himself. The capital letter P is simple and unobtrusive, as the humble poor themselves.

'Remember the Poor' was an injunction to be impressed on the mind of the community in general, as everyone should help those who have less than themselves. It was no pious word, but a practical piece of advice, based on the scriptures.

'Remember the Pore' is carved on the poor-box of many a church, and there it stands in Buckinghamshire villages to this day with the spelling which makes one realize that the pronunciation was different from that we use now. The command was the subject of sermons, the core of stories for children, and even in Victorian days it was a sad little refrain that accompanied the jingling of an alm's-box, the shaking of an empty hat beside a beggar's stand. Pennies were taken from our money-boxes for the poor, the beggars and the gypsies who came to the door. 'Remember the Poor' was an important part of life, and country people helped those with very little as they in turn were helped by the richer ones, for poor is a relative term.

In the eighteenth century and earlier the burden of the poor was carried mainly by alms and charities, and it was designed as far as possible for the poor of the particular parish. It was administered by the parish overseers through the church. From the account books, preserved in the archives of the church, a light shines on the lives of the common people, with their anxieties and difficulties and poverty. Every detail is entered in ink for the scrutiny of the churchwardens.

The widows are there, in the long lists through the centuries, and the lot of the widow was hard when there were no pensions. although much was done for the parishioners to alleviate their burden of children, rents, clothes and food.

There are charges for buryings, for journeys, for doctors' bills, for vagrant money, and the nursing of poor destitute women. Stackwood was bought by the Overseers for their fires, charges for lying-in of women were paid, for there was no hospital. Widows' rents came out of the fund, constables' bills, the charge for 'a boy with ye smal Pox', and 'Paid to 2 Begars' and 'Paid to Joseph Allen's wife for making a shift.'

The hand-writing of those who made the entries is clear and neat, with fine capitals, never ornate, and very small letters evenly formed, as bright and plain as black print. The effect of the upstrokes and downstrokes, the curls and points of letters, almost resembles that of lace-stitch or embroidery spread closely over the long narrow pages. It is the Humanistic writing of the sixteenth century, changed but still retaining the characteristics of that earlier script, and beautiful in its passage through time. Even in this book the writing deteriorates towards the end, it becomes larger, and less regular and delicate.

There is never a blot or erasion, and no alterations mar the tenure of the pages through the century, but the writing changes each year as different scribes took on the task and the spelling of many words changes with each man. One of the words which seems to afford difficulty is 'Beggar' which has several varieties.

Through the years the accounts go on, with nothing spectacular, for this is a simple village—yet one can see the everyday troubles of illness and poverty, of wandering vagrants and scamps. Payments for clothing is a frequent item, and wood for fires, but coal is never mentioned, for this village must have had plenty of wood for gathering, and much stackwood from cut trees.

There are the usual burials of beggars, and accounts for removals of men and women to places outside the parish. Vagrants were returned to their own parishes, as it was not possible to care for them in an adopted parish which had enough to do to maintain its own poor. Each parish was a kingdom to itself as far as poor relief went. There was a continual flow of travelling men and women, beggars and gypsies, who were moved on from parish to parish. A horse goes to Buckingham, probably to take an official or to escort a removal to that town, and the cost is six shillings. There are many bills for the hire of horses.

One item which occurs with embarrassing frequency, is 'Lost by our Rates that Could not be Collected'. This bald statement covers so much—the perplexed collectors, the balancing of accounts which refused to balance, the discussions and arguments and struggles of the Overseers before they confessed and wrote down their bad debts. Charges for 'Going to Law about a Widow' were the large sum of £17 7s., a sum we could multiply by ten to get the modern equivalent. Happily the law is seldom invoked, for it was an expense that was avoided at all costs by country people.

'Given to a Travelling Woman' is a frequent charge on these accounts, for these poor beggars walked from one village to another, collecting their dues, and each village was glad to pay and get rid of them.

'Three Travelling Women' pretended to be in travail, and they got six shillings. One imagines they were bundled quickly away to get their babies elsewhere before the fraud was discovered and the Overseers became the subject for ribald jests.

'A Travoler that was found Dead' cost £2 5s. 6d., which would include removal, burial and inquiries into his death, but it is a large sum, and behind it may lie a tragic story.

Money is spent on nursing the poor and a woman was nursed for four weeks at a cost of £1 14s. 6d.

'Mrs Brown's bill for cureing poor people' is £1 15s., and we wonder about the healing powers of Mrs Brown, who was fetched instead of the doctor to bring her herbs and home-made ointments and salves, her simples and her teas of camomile and rue, of wormwood and yarrow, to cure the ills of these poor people. Her charges were low and she must have treated many people efficiently for the sum of £1 15s. This nursing and healing was a small and wonderful part of village life which is seldom mentioned in period books. In every village these wise helpful women dwelt, and even in Victorian days they carried on their good work. They had healing hands, and a knowledge of the use of herbs. Some of these women lived in the villages I knew in childhood, and they were called in to help in cases where a doctor was too expensive, and a trained nurse out of the question. They gathered eye-bright from the hills and made a decoction from the juices for sore eyes. They grew plants in their cottage gardens, bergamot, with its loose crimson flowers, mullein, elecampane, and Madonna lilies whose petals were used for staunching blood. A Buckinghamshire man whom I know had a cruel wound from a chisel, which slipped and entered his arm, cured by leaves and petals of Madonna lily bound upon the place, at once, with no delay. This was important when doctors were far away.

'Eliz. Brown for Cureing Mary Wingroves Finger, 2/6' we read, and it is written with a flourish and a very large beautiful capital F for the important finger which this famous Mrs Brown cured. Did she use Madonna lily, or a poultice of plantain, the cure-all, or betony, which has a great reputation, or an ointment of goose-grease? We do not know, but she must have been a good healer to be chosen and paid by the Overseers for helping the poor.

Bleeding a woman is 6d. Curing the Widow's family of the Itch is 2s. 6d, and again I think these cures must have been made by Mrs Elizabeth Brown, as the doctor's fees were high.

'Given to Dan Miller to pay ye Chirurgion, £2-2-0' is an item, and doctors were paid in guineas as now, not in odd little sixpences.

There are charges for washing old men, and 16s. is the cost of one man's ablution, so this must have been a disagreeable task with years of dirt to be removed.

A child's coffin is 1s., and burying a vagrant child is 1s., pathetic entries for the unwanted.

Shirts were made for the poor, for 2s. 6d.

A pair of shoes is 4s., which is an expensive item, perhaps about £2 of our money. Shoes were made in a village near, where there is still a tannery for leather and a boot factory of long lineage.

1s. is paid to buy 'the boy' breeches, but someone else has a pair made for 3s.

Thatching a house is 5s., which seems very little, but probably this did not include straw. Cornfields cover many acres of land in this fertile place, under the woods, and there would be plenty of thatching straw available.

'Paid for straw and workmanship', is another thatching item in 1735, for which the Overseers paid £4 2s. 6d. I heard a short time ago of an outbuilding in the same county which a friend wished to have thatched to match her cottage. The price demanded for this small place was £80.

A 'Joynt of Mutton' is 1s., and 'Beer for a Funeral', is 2s. 6d. Funeral Beer is a frequent charge and sometimes it is 5s.

'Given to Peter Child for bread and cheese, 1/4'.

'Paid for Redeeming James East's bed, 8/-'.

'Paid for A Book, three shill-ings' is an item one would like to know more about. What was the Book bought by the Overseers out of their account money? Sermons, herbal, a book of Law? It is the only outlay on a book, and it was not an account book or a church register, for these impor-tant books with their parchment and vellum must have cost much more, nor were they even half filled at the time of the outlay.

'Given to 2 Beggars 2s' is the next item, a frequent one. Again comes the apologetic insertion in the accounts which is so pleasant to read nowadays, for it has a modern familiar air.

'1724. Expenses at several times in and about our Office, 5 shillings and sixpence.'

This is the first time the important word 'office' has been used, and the Overseers are increasing in status.

Schooling for Sarah Higgins is 5s. 6d., an interesting piece of news for Sarah must have been an intelligent little girl to have money spent on her education by the Overseers, when a penny a week was the fee for a Dame's School.

'Paid for putting a boy apprentice, £2-2-6' is another educa-tional fee, a high one for a craftsman in the making.

'Given to a Great Bellyed Woman, 5/-' is a reminder that the woman had to be hurried to the next parish before her child was born to be an additional expense to the small struggling village.

Clothes for the poor are mentioned with regularity, and £4 is paid many times—another interesting statement, for evidently these vagrants and poor were not clothed always in cast-off garments, but in new clothes.

A list of 'Clothes delivered to the Poor', includes the following. 'Robert Williams, a fine shirt for Sundays. Ann Child's girl, 2 shifts, 2 pairs of stockings, a Petticoat.'

There is a note after this, 'Same girl hired to John Hill, Taplow for a year. Her time to be out, April 12.'

More follows about the family, for Ann Child caused some trouble, and there are several mentions of her name.

'To Ann Child, a gown and petticoat which I hear she has sold because she did not like the colour.'

Poor Ann Child, with her daughter in service in Taplow, and she with her delight in colour struggling against the dour masculine choice of her dull clothes. One hopes she got a pretty dress with the money.

'Paid for yarn and knitting Fryor's boy's stockings and expenses when he run from his master, 3/-'—and another story is half-revealed of the troubles of the Overseers against the independent villagers.

A mysterious item is a 'Payement for Snacking', and another is 'Four Turkey Slaves.'

'Paid for Writing, £2-0-0' occurs now and then, but I do not think it refers to the script in the account book, for the names of the Overseers are given at the end of each session, farmers and men of the village, and each signature is boldly written in good lettering and fine style, with pride in the individual handwriting, and in the originality of each capital letter. It makes one envious of the freedom in their writing, their lovely capture of a letter for their own use. A capital A with a device in the centre of the circle like a curled asp is here, and this way of writing the letter was taught to me when I was six years old, by a woman who gave me private lessons. When I went to school it was mocked at and forbidden, and forgotten until I recognized it in the early eighteenth century script.

These slender links even through a capital letter, bring back to life the individualism, the vitality of these people who once lived in the village. Lacemakers, maltsters, labourers, farmers, and 'wheelers', they lived in the village paying their rates, and helping the poor vagrants, the travellers, the beggars and the women with child.

XII

Flowers in Buckinghamshire

The windy flower-sprinkled Chiltern hills, the cherry orchards in the villages, the great woods of beech trees, majestic and straight-limbed, the narrow lanes alight with traveller's joy, spindleberry and dogwood, all are beautiful as flowers themselves, and as richly filled with colour. In early spring when the blackthorn carries snow-white petals on its dark angular branches, so thickly covered that the tree looks like a ghost standing in the moonlight, and in autumn when the beech is tawny-gold and the cherry leaves are crimson and amber, there is a wealth of obvious beauty, but it is down close to the earth that the loveliest small things flourish.

This is a county of wild flowers, for it has not yet been trimmed and shaped to tidiness, and there is some individuality left in the winding lanes and the straggling irregular fields with their mixed hedges, sometimes overgrown, sometimes layered into symmetry by a village craftsman with his hook.

Flowers grow even by the sides of the main traffic roads, where wide green margins are left for the safety of the foot-traveller. There in the deep grass are white pools of dog-daisies, and drifts of innocent bird's-eye—(the little shining speedwell which seems larger and more wide-awake here in the south), patches of blue pennies of wild geranium, and hot golden broom, all displayed along the broad highways where the lorries, cars and buses stream past. By the side of the main road to London I found little clusters of mountain cranesbill, hiding in the verge of a steep incline. The delicate pale blue flowers were safe, for nobody had time to look at them rising from their dark-green foliage. The orange hawk-weed also grows on the bank of this road, the flower we call 'Grim-the-Collier', for it has coal-black hairs. The colour is striking and rich, deep orange-copper, and the flowers grow in bunches on the head of a long dusky-haired stalk.

Near the towns on the waste places small flowers hide the scars. Rose-coloured marjoram, silky musk-mallow, Our Lady's bedstraw, and wild thyme weave a tight net of colour which

spreads round the feet of the hoardings and covers the raw slashes of road excavations, as if in protest. They will not leave their birthplace for any navvies working there. As long as the earth lasts they will return, for they are immortal.

Many of the narrow roads and winding lanes have green verges and ditches under the hedges. The hollows of these damp places are lined with a galaxy of flowers, with wild hyacinths, dog mercury, wood spurge, cuckoo pint, and stitchwort in spring, and myriads of scented white violets grow on the banks. Later on the sulphur-yellow toadflax, stiff aromatic yarrow, pink and cream and pale fawn, and the magenta-rose fringed flowers of the great knapweed stand proudly in the grasses. 'Paint-brush' is the country name for this Rembrandt flower, which is not unlike an outspread brush dipped in purple magenta paint.

The high hedgerows bordering the lanes grow from varied trees, maple and dogwood, ash and oak, hazel and sloe, with here a crab-apple and there a white beam, here a spindleberry, there a wild rose. Over the trees are festooned the delicate grey feathers of traveller's joy, the rich red berries of bitter-sweet and long trails of black bryony like rare jewels in the hedge. Old red brick farms with long low cowhouses and great barns, cornfields golden with wheat and barley, all waiting for the harvest, lie beyond the fruitful flowery hedgerows.

By the lanes are clumps of marjoram, murry-coloured, purple and rose, like garden flowers in their compact neat growth, and musk-mallow with its thin silk skirts of pale pink, sweetly scented, and twisted slender buds. There are the tall spires of the great mullein, a flower that always fascinates me so that I have to stop and consider its purple eye, its yellow velvet petals, and its soft flannel leaves. The leaves can be boiled in milk for a herbal drink, I am told, and the flowers make a hair-wash that is golden. The main stem of this splendid plant has many smaller mulleins growing from it, like yellow candles in the shadows of the ditch. Once I stood beside the flowers, and a nightingale began to sing overhead.

I loiter along these grass-edged lanes to discover fresh beauties in the individual blossoms, for each flower is distinct and different and each seems to contain a secret I may find. Here are the slender fingers of agrimony, like tiny holly-hocks, and near them the tall lovely goat's-beard. The long pointed buds, sharp as a woodcock's bill, the delicate grass-fine leaf springing in a curve from the stalk, the eight green bracts pointing from behind the yellow rays of petals of the flower-head make a decorative design. Most important of all, the round clock of cream and buff seeds, each with a concave pappus like a miniature saucer, is geometrically satisfying. It is a mathematical flower made out of circles and straight lines. I examine it as if I had never seen its beauty before, but I discovered it for myself when I was a child, straying in the forbidden mowing-grass of our own fields. It is called ' John-go-to-bed-at-noon', and off to sleep it goes, shutting its golden eye at midday, as all farm boys used to remember. It was not common on our land, but in Buckinghamshire crowds of these exquisite clocks are held up to the noonday sun, to strike the silent hour of noon.

One August Bank Holiday when I was seeking these goat's-beard clocks to carry away, for the globe of the clock keeps its little parasol heads intact unless the wind is strong, I met a procession all shining gold and yellow so that at first I thought it was a circus coming down the lane under the arching trees. Five great wagons, newly painted canary-yellow with scarlet wheels, were drawn by five splendid cart horses, bay, dapple-grey, and black. Their waving manes were adorned with tassels and ribbons, and more ribbons were plaited in their tails. Horse-brasses and bells jingled musically, and the carters, smiling and waving their beribboned whips, drove slowly along from an agricultural show. None of them had won a prize, but they deserved a first-class for their beauty as they moved along that lane in the evening sunlight, with flecks of gold dust and silver light dripping from the wet trees upon the harness and polished flanks of the horses. They were radiant as the horses of the sun-god himself, and for some reason they were part of the simple beauty of the weeds I sought.

One of the loveliest flowers is the bee orchis, which grows in many places in the county. I found it first at Jordans, where it grew richly in a field. Near Penn there was a haunt of the bee orchis, and village children picked bunches for their mothers, but the field was ploughed up for corn and the flowers disappeared. I found it again on the banks of an old chalk pit, with rosy sainfoin. I thought I saw two bees on a stalk and I stopped to blow them away, when I realized it was the orchis, with dark mottled lip, mauve petal and the brilliant green ribbon. I had been deceived by the mimicry, which preserves the plant. Half hidden in the long grass, a hive of growing bees were the flowers.

The flowers of the chalk have a special miniature charm. Horseshoe vetch, squinancy-wort, rampion, pyramidal orchis,

and the little blue gentian, all grow on the chalk hills, and lady's fingers are entangled in the chalky stones with scarlet, gold and tawny finger-tips. The golden-yellow rockrose holds up its small flowers and slender buds to the sun, it curves its stalk like a dancer, so that I expect it to leap upward. Its roots seek the small stones, while the little blue butterflies hover over it in the heat.

The tiny flowers of the milkwort are treasures, they have such diverse colours. One can find pink and purple, mauve and magenta, deep blue, azure, and snow-white flowers growing near one another in a tapestry of minute pattern. The field scabious which is prolific and strong-growing, has varied shades of lavender blue, dark purple and amethyst in its flower heads. Every flower is different, and on the round pincushions hover the six-spotted Burnet moths. Sometimes a crowd jostles on one flower, with brilliant wings swinging as the moths push for a place. I have seen seven Burnets on one flower head.

One can find the clustered bell-flower, growing on the hills close to the ground, and the green-winged orchis whose reddish-purple flowers have little green wings to adorn them. Sometimes this flower is palest pink or rose, and when I found one nearly white I made my wish over it as all good country people must.

Flowers in Buckinghamshire

The early purple orchis and the marsh orchis grow in the fields, or did until recently when there has been much building on the land. The gypsy women, who know where everything lives, gather the flowers and fill their large baskets, and offer them for sale. Gypsies and ploughing are the destroyers of the orchis family. Even the willows are stripped and broken for the silver palms at Easter. The gypsies always remove the horny scales from the palm willows to enhance the beauty of the silver drops.

Cowslips grow in many places, on railway banks, under hedges, and in fields. There is one field where they are tall and splendid as if they are garden flowers, with oxlips among them, and many a hanging bell on each thick stalk. Primroses are less plentiful, and I find them in a wood where a stream runs, for the fields seem to be too dry for these early flowers.

Succory, or chicory, fringes the cornfields, on high land and low. The starry flowers with their ragged petals, blue as the sky above, radiant as the zenith on a summer's day, grow to full height and beauty on the chalk. They twinkle and give out a light of their own, I sometimes think. The tough stems are hard to break, and the plant is a source of trouble in the corn, but it keeps to the verges of the fields, close to the footpath or by the gates. It is a 'keeper of the way', a flower that likes company, one of those friendly flowers which seem to seek human society. Many branches spring from the main stem, each with its blossoms, and the chicory is a candelabra with blue lights burning. The flower heads wither and curl up, while others open out and new buds unfold. So there are full blown flowers, buds and withered petals on the same stalk.

Coral-root grows in certain places, and in one wood there are quantities of this uncommon flower, which I found with joy, for it was new to me. The lavender flowers have a secret beauty, and the stalks themselves and leaves with finely cut edges, all are attractive. The little dark beads in the axils, and the pink coral root give the name to the flower, for the plant grows lightly, near the surface of the leaf mould in the shade of deep woods.

Tansy, less common here than in the north, fills the air with pungent odour in some of the rough pastures or by the sides of roads. The cattle leave it alone, perhaps because the taste is bitter. The flat gold buttons clustered tightly together on stems two or three feet high are beautiful in their own way. The feathery foliage spreads out like ferns. I am prejudiced in favour of tansy, whose distinctive smell is evocative of simple people and country life, and I always carry off a piece to rub in my fingers for the smell. Mugwort, too, grows in luxuriance in the lanes, silver-grey, beaded and tall.

One spring day I saw a golden flood of kingcups in a rushy meadow on the banks of the elusive little river Misbourne. The Misbourne is a river that has the habit of disappearing and then returning, and the kingcups are small or large according to the water around them. I climbed the stone wall and walked in the boggy field to gaze at the beauty before me, a north country beauty. The water reflected the blue sky, and the flowers were like a drift of solid gold in the emerald-green grass. I gathered an armful, I felt greedy for this fairy gold which I had not touched for years, but my inroad made no difference. The thick hollow stalks carried high the large bright leaves, and the glittering flowers and fat buds were nearly as large as yellow water-lilies. Such kingcups I had never seen before. They were finer than the north country flowers, they were cups of burnished metal, reflecting every ray of the sun. I took them home and they lasted many days in a great bowl of water. Another time, in this same place, I found the river bordered with yellow monkey-flower, which grew in the water at one of its shallow periods.

St John's wort, harebells, and spiny pink rest-harrow all

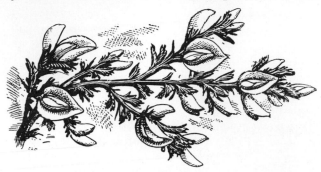

decorate the sides of the lanes, while honeysuckle holds up its cream coronets above the hedges. I was taken to a honeysuckle wood, far away in the Chiltern hills, and the sight of the flowers was breath-taking. The trees were wreathed in honeysuckle, they were white and cream, with myriads of the scented flowers, and to walk among them was a continual amazement at the luxuriance, tropical in its beauty. There were such masses of flowers as I never believed could exist in England, and the scent that filled the air was sweetness itself.

Bugle lies like a blue shadow in the lanes, and the rich deep colour of the trusses rising above the blue-green leaves always makes me stop and stare in contemplation of this simple unnoticed flower. Alkanet with its forget-me-not eye appears in some villages, under the walls, and comfrey with white flower-bells grows on the commons and by the Thames, where one can find the tall orange balsam, the American balsam, as well as the pink balsam, whose curling pods shoot out seeds with startling effect.

In the cornfields the corncockle grows, an unwelcome but

attractive visitor. In the steep lane near I found a giant corn-cockle, nearly five feet high, with large purple-magenta flowers of great beauty. Another time I came across a red cowslip growing under a hedge, far from any habitation. The orpine, or livelong, grows in these shady lanes, with fleshy leaves and curving flower. The old name is Midsummer-men, for the flower was used in magical practices on Midsummer Eve. The tall nettle-leaved bell-flower stands by the hedge, with blue flowers ringing down the stalk, and this flower always gives me great pleasure. Wild Canterbury bell we called it, for it grew in our deserted quarries. In a certain wood in Mid-Bucks the bell-flowers are white, like ghosts in the shadow, and very beautiful they look.

I have never found the Pasque flower which grows in the county in secret places, nor the purple-flowering daphne. My woodman sees the daphne when he cuts trees near Stokenchurch. An old man told me that when he was a boy he used to find hundreds growing in the woods. He pulled them up and sold them for a penny each. I am content with the garden variety of the daphne which flowers in February in my garden.

White helleborine grows in a wood near the track of the prehistoric Grim's Ditch. It has the delicacy of a lily, and I felt very happy to see this beautiful flower which I had long wished to find. Green hellebore, a strange flower, seems bewitched to me, perhaps because all green flowers have something magical about them. Even the woody spurge has the same mystery of earth and underworld. Blue periwinkle carpets the ground in one of the Buckinghamshire woods, and there the evergreen leaves and deep blue flowers lie bathed in the shadow of the beech trees, making a wonderful stretch of colour as the sun points long fingers down.

There is a hill where it is easy to believe in witchcraft and ancient gods, and on its slopes I found two distinguished flowers which enchanted me, each in its own way, one in awe, one in beauty. I went to Cymbeline's Mount, the British earthwork, which has traditions of the battle in which Cymbe-

line's sons were slain. It is a haunted spot, and the air is cold
here, even on a summer day, and a little wind rustles the grass
and lifts the leaves when everywhere is still. Ghosts seem to
wander up and down, restless and lost. On the summit of the
grassy mound inside the steep rampart grew a branching
tree—but it was not a tree. It was the deadly nightshade, whose
many outstretched arms carried dark dim jewels of berries and
dull purple bells. It was sinister and beautiful in that place of
traditional death. It was alive and waiting and I was glad I was
not alone with it. In an old herbal the list of 'Poysons' includes
mandrake, nightshade, henbane, and wolfsbane, a deadly
quartet. Many people confuse the bitter-sweet—the woody
nightshade—with the deadly nightshade, but bitter-sweet is
an everyday charming plant, with purple and yellow flowers,
which swing and dance on the hedges.

We climbed the upper part of the hill above the Mount of
Cymbeline, picking the pyramidal orchis, delicate pink spires,
walking on a narrow chalk track which winds through an
ancient wood of bent, leaning, twisted box trees. The scent of
those trees ravished my heart, for the burning sun brought out
the full strength of the odours, and the smell of box is something a country person carries through life. Above on the bare
hillside was a blaze of hot blue light, a broad patch of dazzling
colour unlike that of any flowers I knew. We scrambled across
the narrow valley and found the bushes of viper's bugloss, of
immense size and perfect beauty. It was the day, the hour of
their perfection, and they held out long trails of transparent
glassy blue, purple and pink bells to that scorching sky, with
the wide plain of Aylesbury stretched below in its soft layers
of lavender and misted blue.

About twenty years ago two marshy fields, each of five acres,
near the village of Ford, were completely carpeted in early May
with the delicate chequered bells of fritillaries. The local name
for the flower is frog-cup, or fra'-cup, as the mottled petals
remind country people of a frog's back. On the gate to these
enchanting meadows was a collecting box, where pickers of the

flowers on the first Sunday in May, 'Fra'-cup Sunday', put a donation for the Aylesbury hospital. Now these thousands of fritillaries are lost for ever.

I came home the other day with an autumnal bunch I picked in a lane, in a tangle of hedge and road banks. There were blue sloes, with the bloom on the fruit, crab-apples from a tree which carried more crabs than leaves, crimson aiges from a hawthorn, yellow mullein spires, deep purple and pale mauve scabious, marjoram, pink and mulberry-coloured, wild mignon-ette, and the silver seed-cases of the knapweed. With these I had gathered the transparent ruby berries of the bitter-sweet, the sulphur-yellow toadflax, rosy leaves of wild cherry and orange-pink berries of the spindle. Lighting up this golden bouquet of autumn were branches of late chicory, with its tender blue stars. It was an epitome of England herself, strong beautiful, harsh, enduring, with flowers and fruit of immortal names.